WHOSE HOUSEWORK IS IT ANYWAY?

FIONNUALA HAYDEN

First published in 1995 by
Marino Books
An imprint of Mercier Press
16 Hume Street Dublin 2

Trade enquiries to Mercier Press
PO Box 5, 5 French Church Street,
Cork

A Marino Original

© Fionnuala Hayden 1995 text and
illustrations

ISBN 1 86023 012 1

10 9 8 7 6 5 4 3 2 1

A CIP record for this title is available
from the British Library

Cover design by Cathy Dineen
Illustrations by the author
Set by Richard Parfrey
Printed in Ireland by ColourBooks,
Baldoyle Industrial Estate, Dublin 13

WHOSE HOUSEWORK IS IT ANYWAY?

FIONNUALA HAYDEN

CONTENTS

INTRODUCTION

Agony aunts write: 'If you pay too much attention to your spotless home, your partner may fall into the arms of the first good-natured slob who comes along'. *Whose Housework Is It Anyway?* is for good-natured slobs, men and women, who do not want their partner to fall into the arms of the first spotless housekeeper who comes along.

It is also for all home sharers, including everybody's children.

It does not take twice as long to have a clean, smooth-running home. The opposite is the case. Once get your home and systems set up to be easy to run, and the daily and weekly running will take less time and effort.

Less total time and effort. But also less 'one-person' time and effort.

Because worldwide, women still carry most of the housework burden. This is whether they live in industrialised countries or not, have children or not, are in employment (full- or part-time) or not.

It's an idea whose time has gone. Everyone doing their fair share is an idea whose time has come.

Whose Housework Is It Anyway? says what is a fair share to ask. Shows how to ask it. And tells beginners how to do it. It offers equal opportunities in housework to men, women and children.

The three themes of *Whose Housework Is It Anyway?* are:

- How to do the housework efficiently
  For complete beginners, there are how-to and how- not-to instructions. Until now, in one million homes, one million women tried to explain about housework to one million men and over two million children. Now *Whose Housework Is It Anyway?* can act as a self-training manual.
- How to set up an easy-to-run home
  Get most results for least effort.
- How to share the housework
  Homes don't want everybody doing whatever is asked whenever it's asked. They want it done without asking. The housework black belt to yellow belt divisions neatly sum up four levels of housework contribution. Just choose your belt and a clear group of housework tasks is yours.

Beginners welcome, no experience needed!

Whose Housework Is It Anyway? contains everything you ever wanted to tell your partner, children or house-mates about housework. Only, this is clearer, shorter and more polite!

1
ARE YOU A HOUSEWORK BLACK BELT?

Most housework tasks take between one and twenty minutes. No, don't stop reading. It's true. Vacuuming a room, clearing a meal, tidying your bedroom, ironing three shirts and a pants – any of these tasks can be done in less than twenty minutes.

Housework seems never-ending because there are so many of these tasks to do. They need to be done at different times of the day and in different parts of the home. Housework does not consist of one long task. It's a collection of very many short or shortish tasks.

This makes it ideal for many helpers.

BEGINNER'S YELLOW BELT

This will take less than ten minutes a day per person, a minute here and there. Age six and upwards qualify for the yellow belt. It's largely the kinds of things that you would do out of courtesy if visiting someone else's home. Your own home needs them also.

Clear away after your own snack, keep your belongings tidy, make your bed. Flush the toilet and leave the bathroom as clean as you found it, leave cupboard doors and drawers closed, put dirty clothes in the laundry basket, put clean clothes back in the press. You open a

CHILDREN, I DON'T KNOW HOW TO SAY THIS.
PLEASE DON'T MISUNDERSTAND.
THIS MAY SOUND LIKE A COMPLAINT. IT IS!

cupboard to grab something and something else falls out. Put it back. You knock down a bike in the garage. Pick it up.

You've heard of DIY. This is CIY: clear-it-yourself, clean-it-yourself.

These tasks are time-sensitive and need to be done immediately they arise by the person on the spot, the person who triggers them. If this is done straight away, then the place looks OK for the longest possible time.

Does that mean that you cannot enjoy a snack unless you clear away after? That you have to put away your coat and sports gear when you come in? Yep. Who else is going to do it, and when? You're on the spot. You've created the one-minute task. Spend the one minute at it. There's never the same momentum if it's left until later.

YELLOW BELT PROFICIENCY TEST

Know how to make and serve one meal. Starting from now, choose one meal and learn how to produce it. Practise on friends. Nobody will be too critical at the beginning. This is a serious requirement; you never know when it will be needed.

OK guys, that's almost it. That's the beginner's yellow belt. Tidy habits. Clear as you go. Become expert at making one meal. It's not going to hurt. After a few months it becomes automatic and no burden.

That's 'almost' it?

Meal clear-away gets a special mention here because very few eaters realise just how much time this takes. Even if a good bit of the clear-up has been done during preparation. Even in a home where eaters carry their own table settings and load them into a dishwasher, the remaining kitchen clear-up could take a solo worker thirty-five minutes. So the fairest suggestion is this: all finish together. All eaters finish all the clearing away at the same time. There are variations on this if there are many of you. Perhaps the preparer(s) are excused the clearing up. Or the clearing-up is done before the coffee. At all costs, there are two things to be avoided: a solo clear-up after a communal meal and a postponed clear-up.

GREEN BELT

Green belts do the yellow belt stuff plus laundering their own things. Eleven-year-old Steve is a green belt. 'This is much better, me doing my own laundry,' he says. 'At least now if I need something clean in a hurry, I can be sure of having it, since I wash it myself.'

Green belts also keep their bedrooms tidy and look after their own towels and bed linen. They change the sheets, wash them and return them to storage in their own bedrooms ready for the next change.

Anyone who can pre-set a video recorder for five different programs on four different TV channels fourteen days in advance, as nine-year-olds can, is capable of doing a wash, dry and fold-away of clothes.

GREEN BELT PROFICIENCY TEST

Become expert at washing and ironing your own things.

PURPLE BELT

Purple belts do the green belt stuff plus some rostered housework: about twenty minutes daily and one to three hours extra during the week.

And they also run their own errands. No 'Would you mind popping over to Gerry's to fetch my gear for the weekend' stuff. If you were sharing with friends or colleagues, you would not expect one of them to do your laundry, run your errands or clean up after you.

PURPLE BELT PROFICIENCY TEST

Clean a bathroom properly and thoroughly with no shirking the difficult bits.

BLACK BELT

The black belt is where the buck stops. Black belts do the planning, setting up – and worrying. They organise rosters and supervise green, yellow and purple belts.

Black belts *do* the housework: they notice whatever has to be done and do it, messy or not, lengthy or not, without being reminded or said please and thank you to. They decide and take overall responsibility for organising the best solutions for the home and for child arrangements. Both for every day and for emergencies.

With two black belts, a good way to share the worries and responsibilites is to divide them according to the main housework categories:

- Tidy/clean
- Meals
- Laundry
- Childcare
- Entertaining

It's a bit like the way a hotel functions, whereby the cleaning staff operates separately from the kitchen staff, and the laundry can be isolated from the other functions. But homes need multi-skilled people, not specialists in just one task, so swop around responsibilities regularly.

You don't want household members to do whatever you ask whenever you ask. You want them to do it without being asked. That's why everyone needs to choose what YGPB belt they'll be: yellow, green, purple or black.

The minimum is yellow belt. This is largely clear-it-yourself, clean-it-yourself, those half-minute to two-minute tasks that arise throughout the day throughout the home.

CLEAR-IT-YOURSELF, CLEAN-IT-YOURSELF

CIY means that whoever causes these short tasks, does them. It's terrific value for the time spent. A one-minute clearance after your own snack is worth double that time if someone else had to do it instead – because someone else isn't on the spot (as you are).

Plus, if you do it immediately it leaves the place looking good for the longest possible time.

Many people are astonished to learn that a tiny child can have a vocabulary of many hundreds of words. It is with the same astonishment that we learn a fact about housework tasks. While people are moving around their home, preparing a meal, preparing to go out, switching from one activity to the next, there can be over one hundred opportunities per hour to do a short task or portion of a task. Or not to do it! To do it or to shirk it.

Hang up your cardigan or leave it slumped on the floor. Put the empty crisp packet in the waste basket – or leave it on the chair. Bring your snack things to the kitchen or leave them on the floor by the TV. Wash up your snack things or do not wash them. Dry them and put them away or leave them draining.

If all opportunities to shirk are availed of, it adds up to a big backlog per person. If there is more than one shirker, the home deteriorates very quickly.

These are not tasks that need decisions. We're talking about much less than a minute per task. These are occasions for automatic action, opportunistic swipes at tasks as they arise.

Homes really need everyone to realise that the task belongs to the activity that gives rise to it and to the person who carries out the activity. The task does not belong to mother.

2
SET UP AN EASY-TO-RUN HOME

The easy-to-run home is set up for self-service. It should be as straightforward as a self-service cafeteria or launderette. No cute improvisations that only one person can work. It should be possible for housework to be done well by ordinary people. No extraordinary effort should be needed.

This does not mean that everything has to cost a fortune. It just means setting up systems and methods that are efficient and clear.

Self-service means that communal tasks are easy to do and to share and personal tasks are easy for individuals to do for themselves.

Don't expect to set it up overnight. Like organising a data base, there's a bit of work in setting it up. But ever afterwards, it's quick and easy to use. Running a home does not consist of moving mountains every day. It consists of moving mountains once only (set up your home to be easy to run) and then moving molehills every day afterwards – each person moving their own molehill!

DECENTRALISE
These days, living space is getting smaller because of expense. But the number of personal belongings is increasing. Practically every man, woman and child has

THE EASY-TO-RUN HOME

Pretty important
- Decentralise
- No clutter or junk
- Deal with garbage

Important
- Exit/entry area
- Paperwork
- Message/information area
- The home's on/off controls
- Every home should have one . . .
- Household linen
- Cleaning cupboard

Very important
- Storage
- Equipment
- Ten of the best convenience features

at least one sports holdall with sports equipment, in addition to personal stereos, books and magazines.

The central area of homes, the hall/livingroom/kitchen, cannot handle all these items, constantly on the move, often left on surfaces. To decentralise them is the only answer. Unless you have plenty of space in a utility area, plan space for them in the bedrooms.

Then it will be possible to have as a house rule: no personal belongings scattered in communal areas because it affects everyone else's use and enjoyment of the place. Scattered and abandoned items will be dumped into an all-purpose tidy-up container or confiscated for a period.

Another fairly recent development is that we take showers more often, using more towels than before. A bathroom may not have enough towel rail for several people's towels. A rail in the bedroom is an answer, with each person bringing their towel to the bathroom and back. This cuts down on towel use (or misuse!).

We also expect clean clothes more often than we did ten years ago. And the central area cannot handle laundry-in-transit either.

An extra role for bedrooms is what we're looking at. Yes, I know that bedrooms are small; that shared bedrooms can be a problem; that it's a chore to go upstairs with belongings the minute you come in. And that it's challenging to set up such a bedroom. But the alternative is too many belongings in the communal area.

If they are in communal areas, they become a communal management problem. Ingredients: overall clutter, nagging, mislaid items, one person having to organise for everyone else, more nagging.

If they are in the bedrooms, they are an individual management problem. A bedroom can become a supply, service and replenish depot for each person, supplied, serviced and replenished by that person.

Reader, it works. Not only does it take in-transit belongings and laundry away from central areas, it takes the responsibility for them away from head office. And it does not require heavy instructions or administration. The house rule is simple: please keep your belongings in your bedroom.

Empower everybody to control as much as possible of their own home requirements.

Here is the alarm clock example.

In some homes there is just one alarm clock. Whoever sleeps with it has the job of waking everyone else, of making sure everyone gets up.

But in homes where each person has their own alarm clock, each person manages their own timetable. It makes sense to empower individuals.

No clutter or junk

Clutter consists of too much stuff on surfaces. It can be intentional, for example lots of ornaments and knicknacks. Or unintentional. Clutter is a disaster because it acts as a magnet. 1 clutter + 1 clutter = 3 clutter.

But once you get stuff out of the way, it stays out of the way. It will not be bothering you for days and weeks to come.

First-time apartment dwellers can keep their apartments tidy, largely by leaving all unnecessary items home at mother's. If mother's is not available, leave unnecessary items at the refuse tip. If *you* are mother's, bring your kids' stuff to the refuse tip.

Junk is not the same as clutter. Junk is stuff that is of no use to you.

Four steps, none of them easy, for getting rid of junk:

1 Assemble junk items.
2 Estimate their value if they had to be replaced.
3 Limbo them for four weeks in case you have serious second thoughts.
4 Finally chuck them out.

Throw out stuff. If you buy new items, throw out old items. If you get your hair cut this morning, throw out your hair rollers this afternoon. You need to be constantly discarding things.

Homes may purchase two or three bagfuls of non-food items each week. The same amount has to be discarded each week. Scour your home on the day before bin day for stuff to be discarded.

Spotless housekeepers don't hesitate to meet their time and tidiness targets by chucking in the waste bin instead of painstakingly sorting through bundles. They are prepared to handle items once and once only, either to put away in a designated spot or to chuck.

A GLORY-HOLE, NO. A BREATHING-SPACE, YES.

Have you ever found yourself thinking: 'I should have washed my hair yesterday but I didn't get round to it.' Housework tasks also get postponed. We lead such busy lives that we don't always manage to do everything we would like to do when we wish.

A structured, regularly cleared space for in-transit items or items to be decided on later can give you a breathing space. It's a kind of limbo, a place where unfinished stuff will not be in the way. It can offer a lay-by possibility, perhaps for household laundry or a hobby. Or it can give you time to decide on uncertain items.

Don't let it get overstuffed and out of hand. Inspect and clear it regularly. Lay-by possibilities can be good if not overused. What you don't need is a space where you open the door, close your eyes and chuck 'don't know' things in, never to be retrieved.

GARBAGE

I don't want to hear anybody in the home saying 'What day is bin day?' Garbage is everybody's duty, consisting of:

- emptying each room's waste bin a few times a week
- bagging the kitchen garbage once a day and bringing it to outdoor storage
- once a week putting full bins out for collection and bringing them back in once they've been emptied

For food refuse, outdoor garbage containers need a lid to stop animals getting at it. Non-smelly paper refuse doesn't need a covered bin; it can be in plastic refuse sacks.

Green garbage? Sort garbage into separate categories. For old newspapers, a good idea is a newspaper limbo: yesterday's papers are taken out of circulation but kept for a week before being thrown out, in case anyone wishes to have a second look.

EXIT/ENTRY AREA

This area needs:

- a definite home for keys, hanging hooks or a bowl, but not near enough to the hall door for casual callers to pinch
- space for bags and for assembling things to be taken out next time: dry cleaning, library books, letters to post
- a mirror and clothes brush
- space for coats umbrellas, bags, hats, gloves

Few homes have space in such an area for sports gear, pushchair, large or outdoor toys, wet boots. A locker-sized area per person, as in schools or clubs, would be a great idea for personal gear if you could manage the space for it. If you cannot, designate places for these things elsewhere. But don't tolerate them cluttering up the hall if the hall cannot accommodate them.

If you have hall-door brasses to polish, keep brass polish and cloth in the hall as well as the hall's other cleaning supplies.

Leave a spare key with neighbours in case of necessity.

PAPERWORK

Dealing with paperwork in one place and one place only is the aim. If you have only one rule about paperwork, make it this one: the place where mail is opened and read is the place where it is dealt with, stored, and filed. Try to handle most items of paperwork once only:

- Dump the piece of paper into the wastebasket, which is on the spot.
- Act on it immediately – write a date in your calendar; make a telephone call; write a cheque; address and stamp the envelope.
- File it. Straight into its specific file is good. But if you haven't time to do that, or if you haven't got a specific file for it, put it into a general file for later attention.

A general, rough filing system is better than no filing system. It may even be better than an elaborate but troublesome system that you'll abandon. The type of container is not important. It can be an antique bureau or a plastic bag.

FILES

Your paperwork centre needs one general 'rough' file plus itemised files for:

- personal records: copy cvs, birth certs and so on
- medical records: reports and bills, receipts, innoculation records
- kids' school reports
- your home's on/off controls (see below)
- appliance guarantees and instructions
- car
- holidays
- personal letters to answer in due course
- money: bank, mortgage, bills, receipts

STATIONERY

- address book with birthday dates, special dates
- spare birthday cards, thank-you notes, gift wrapping, stationery, stamps, Christmas card list (received and sent).

MESSAGE/INFORMATION AREA

A notice board can be the focus of your home's message/
information area. It's convenient if it is near the telephone
and the paperwork centre. In this area would be displayed:

- calendar with forthcoming commitments
- items of general household interest
- master shopping list where required items are ticked,
  ready for the next shopping day
- roster for purple and black belt scheduled housework
- un-removable paper pad with pencil attached, for
  incoming telephone messages
- display space for incoming mail and telephone messages.
  It's up to each person to check if there's anything for
  them.

The notice board is for short-term displays only. Don't
allow out-of-date stuff to lodge there.

THE HOME'S ON/OFF CONTROLS

Make sure that everyone over the age of twelve knows
where the following controls are, and how to regulate
them if appropriate. Keep all instructions together in one
file. A formal run-through of instructions is useful, and
may have to be repeated until everyone understands each
control.

- central heating and radiators
- electricity and fuse board
- hot water
- air conditioning

- mains water supply
- home alarm system

Plan a fire drill – escape routes and assembly points

Lock up the home for the night, when going out, or for routine everyday and every night security. Everyone in the home has to buy into security routines. No exceptions.

EVERY HOME SHOULD HAVE ONE

Every home should have one of the following, and a place for it. Family homes with small children, still operating as a single unit, can manage with one of everything, centrally organised. But later on, individual supplies assist independence, self-management and self-service. And cut down on squabbles. So have either one per home in a fixed spot, or (marked *) personal ones for individual use.

- *scissors and *nailscissors, *needles and *threads (plus needles and threads near the laundry area), *writing paper and *stamps, *hairdryer, *clothes brush. Perhaps for anyone who does their own ironing, a personal iron in the bedroom? (Only do this if you are satisfied with the electrical safety aspects.)
- tidy-up-container, perhaps one upstairs, one downstairs as a catch-all for out-of-place belongings. Owners retrieve them from the tidy-up container. If they are abandoned for too long, confiscate them.
- tool kit including general purpose oil, plumbing plunger, glue or adhesive
- medicines, locked or out of children's reach, and a first aid kit

- spares: fuses, plugs, light bulbs, candles, matches, flashlight, toilet rolls, dogfood
- marker (for naming clothes)
- shoe polish
- Every room needs a waste bin and a mini cleaning kit.
- Every bedroom needs a laundry bag or basket and a towel rail if the bathroom is short of space.

HOUSEHOLD LINEN

What to buy, how much of it, how often washed, where stored?

It will be possible for everyone to wash and manage their own, if each person's bedlinen and towels are personal, identifiable and fairly cute. Fairly cute is important so as to stop people migrating to someone else's stuff. And chosen by each individual if possible.

Unmatching, odd bedlinen might be fine when one person is in charge of it all, its washing, storing and allocation. But identifiable sets per bed will enable everyone to take charge of their own: wash it every week and store the clean set in their bedroom ready for the next change. Purchasing time is the opportunity to ensure easy-care items.

BEDLINEN

Two sets of bedlinen per bed is enough, one on the bed, one being washed.

Avoid work! Keep bedding as clean as possible by using mattress covers; underblankets between the bottom sheet and mattress cover. Use pillow protectors under the pillowcase to give extra protection from dribble stains.

TOWELS

Trickier. If they are seen as household items, everyone will help themselves to clean towels as they wish. And nobody will undertake responsibility for washing them. Identifiable personal towels, perhaps four to six per person, gives laundry responsibility to each person. And cuts down on use! If towel-rail space in the bathroom is limited, one solution would be towel-rail space in the bedroom. Everybody would then bring their towel to the bathroom and back. A bit awkward, but without lots of towel-rail in the bathroom, towels will huddle damp on the floor and get only one use before having to be washed again.

Sports towels usually have patterns that are identifiable, and are best washed with the owner's other sports gear.

Towel colours: dark colours can become scoured whitish from washing, pale colours fade to a dirty white and plain colours are very difficult to keep looking spotless. So I always buy patterned towels of medium colour with no white in them.

HOUSEHOLD LINEN STORAGE

Don't store items that are in daily and weekly use with inactive linens. The inactive items might slip into half-hearted circulation, the active items become less accessible.

CLEANING CUPBOARD

You don't want the whereabouts of cleaning stuff to be known by one person only. You want everyone to know where. That's the argument for having a centralised all-purpose cleaning supplies depot.

However your home may not have space for one in a convenient central location. That's one argument for placing a mini cleaning kit in a number of spots throughout the home: a brush and mop in the kitchen, a carpet sweeper and/or vacuum upstairs as well as downstairs, bathroom cleaning kit in each bathroom if you have more than one. The other argument for mini cleaning kits is that they are readily to hand for immediate use whenever a job arises.

Or a carrying-around bucket of cleaning supplies is useful. It needs to live in one spot and to be returned there.

The point is that everyone should know where to find supplies and equipment and where to return them to.

CLEANING CLOTHS

Disposable cloths or kitchen paper are handy. Even ordinary toilet paper is handy in bathrooms as it prevents recirculating bacteria, fluff and hairs, and saves having to wash cleaning cloths thoroughly. Some people use a colour-coded cleaning-cloth system: green for floors, blue for the loo, yellow for dry dusting, red for polishing, pink for damp dusting. Cumbersome but workable if you believe in it.

SHOE POLISH

Put down a sheet of newspaper on which to polish shoes. Fold up and dispose of the newspaper containing mud and polish flecks.

Finally, what you *don't* need in your cleaning cupboard: sports gear, hobbies, old coats, broken lamps. Make it a self-respecting, businesslike cleaning cupboard.

STORAGE

Storage is what you buy in a furniture store, or what the
builder built in. But that's only the shell. Your thinking
input and commitment are just as important.

It doesn't matter whether it's pine or formica or shelves
or drawers. What's essential, if your storage is to be
successful, is that you and everyone in your home bond
with it, and commit to storing certain items in certain
spaces. Dedicate your storage. Computer users say:
rubbish in, rubbish out. It's the same with storage. Put
things away more or less randomly, and the only way they
can be retrieved is more or less randomly. Your responsibility doesn't end with choosing and paying for the
storage in the shop. Once you get it home, you need to
think about it, decide how it is best used, then commit to
those decisions. Perhaps label storage spots, so that
everyone can cooperate with them.

If your storage areas are the right size in the right
place, it takes very little more effort to put things in their
correct place than to leave them out. And the place looks
smashing with things put away.

ACTIVE OR INACTIVE STORAGE?

The aim is that things that are necessary for day to day
jobs and for living are easy to put your hand on, easy to
put away. And everything else is out of the way. Active
items need storage spots that always have empty space.
About one-third empty is good.

Less frequently used items don't need to be so accessible and inactive or dead storage items need to be out of
circulation. Then they will not be in the way or require
cleaning attention. These would be luggage or seasonal

items, baby items, or equipment used in illness.

Storage cuckoos are useless items which take up good storage places. This leaves no room for current items, which have to overflow on to surfaces and into corners.

'One day I realised that there was no room for my toothbrush in the toothbrush holder,' says Geraldine. 'It was full so that I had to leave mine beside the soap. But who did these toothbrushes belong to? Aunt Sal? The guest who stayed last Easter? Somebody's duplicate left over from scout camp?

Storage cuckoos have to go. Don't store useless items. The dump is the place for useless items.

STORAGE: HOW MUCH AND WHERE?

How do you know how much space you will need in two years' time? You don't. But a home cannot keep bringing in more stuff week after week, year after year, and expect it to fit into the original storage. You need to be continually re-assessing and constantly throwing out.

The smaller your home, the bigger the proportion of it that you need to devote to storage. And the smaller your home, the less untidiness and clutter will be tolerable.

3
EQUIPMENT AND CONVENIENCE FEATURES

Don't automatically suppose that you must have everything that you see advertised, or that it would make your life easier. Every item that has loyal supporters also has disappointed users. Take your time choosing. Spend as much as you can afford. Bargains are a delight on the day of purchase but every day afterwards you may regret that you did not buy an item of better quality.

Making a stop-gap purchase until you can afford something better later? If you buy a rock-bottom item, you may have to dump it later. But if you can buy up a notch, you may be able to sell it secondhand when you are finished with it.

How to make your way through the maze of goods on offer? Consumers' associations publish regular magazines containing test results on consumer durables. Libraries keep copies. They are well worth consulting.

For larger purchases you'll probably plan the financing. But for the smaller electric and non-electric home items, you may find that you are trying to finance them out of current income, and they can take a big chunk of it. With the appliances you need a budget for immediate repairs.

Your greatest and unrepeatable opportunity to interest everyone in using an appliance is to involve them in the choice, purchase and running-in of it. This may go against your better judgement. Naturally you want to be first to check it, note and notify any faults. But if you can give first go of it to household members, they will be the ones to read the instructions, and figure it out while its newness causes enthusiasm. *And* you will not become identified as the sole named driver of the thing, the leading actor with the major role, leaving only walk-on parts for others. After all, if it's new, the appliance will still be under guarantee – a much better time for them to banjax it than a year later.

There is a disadvantage in giving everyone access to the washing machine or the shoe polish. Others may not use it as intelligently, economically or carefully as you would do. You know its little quirks, likes and dislikes, and can coax the best out of it. And it's true that a machine with one careful lady owner will have a higher secondhand value than one with many users. But what you need is many users – not a high secondhand value. Turn the machines over to the family.

TEN OF THE BEST CONVENIENCE FEATURES

Convenience features in a home should mean that work can be:

- eliminated altogether
- made quicker or easier to do
- done at a more convenient time
- easier to share

It is difficult to match features or appliances with these aims in advance, until you see them in action. So here are

'Ten of the Best' – ten personal favourite convenience features from people in different domestic situations:

'A continuous plinth at floor level in our kitchen was one of the things I insisted on,' says **Frances**. 'It means that I can sweep or mop the kitchen floor almost with one movement – almost with one hand. No gaps or crevices at counter level either. The continuous counter and plinth meant buying 'built-under' appliances, including an oven built underneath the dropped-in hob. 'It seemed an extravagance at the time,' says Frances, 'but it has made the kitchen so easy to keep clean. No grunge or crumbs accumulate under, beside or behind the fridge or cooker or other appliances.'

Davy and Marianne are the parents of Ruthie (5) and Sean (2). They both work full-time and Marianne's mother comes every day to mind the children. 'It's an ideal arrangement,' says Marianne, 'but my mother goes home at six when one of us returns, so there is still meal clearance and kitchen clearance to be done in the evening.'

Davy and Marianne's favourite aid? 'Three years ago, when it was a choice between buying a new carpet or a dishwasher, we bought a dishwasher. We've never regretted it,' they say.

'But a dishwasher is one of those appliances that requires your cooperation. It's not like an electric blanket or a TV, which is nice to you and expects nothing in return.

'For a start, a dishwasher needs plentiful supplies of crockery and cutlery. And a dishwasher gives of its best if it's run to a regular timetable, so that the household knows its daily deadline. The dishwasher cycle takes an hour or more, so dirty items arriving after the cycle starts cannot be put in. In fact, nothing can be put in until the cycle is finished and everything is emptied. It's not possible to work a half-clean, half-dirty dishwasher.

'Yes, you've spotted the timing challenge: to run the dishwasher at a time when dirty items have stopped arriving; and to empty it promptly so that it's ready for its next batch of dirty dishes.

'Filling and starting the dishwasher usually also entails a frisk of the kitchen. It's convenient if this can be done as part of the evening meal clear-up. But it means that dishes from late meals or snacks need to be hand-washed. Otherwise they lie on the counter overnight and attract mice.'

Satisfy these dishwasher requirements and the appliance will more than satisfy you.

Brendan: 'I bought an extension flex for the vacuum, and it's great. Now I can plug it in and vacuum the whole place at one go. Somehow, it breaks the flow – makes you feel like just doing half of it, if you have to reposition the flex and restart the job. For quick frisks, a non-electric carpet sweeper is very, very handy.'

The family of **Anna and Don** are almost grown up. As newly-weds they and their friends gave elaborate dinner parties. Anna remembers one menu. 'It started with crabmeat salad served in the shell. That was followed by fillet of beef in puff pastry served with allumette potatos, green beans, cauliflower au gratin, horseradish sauce. And

I made two deserts: rum baba and charlotte russe.'

Entertaining took a back seat while their children were young. But recently Anna and Don have started inviting friends again.

'This time around it's totally different,' says Don. 'For a start, we're not using our silver-plated cutlery. That's in the attic. It was just too troublesome to use. The tines of the forks got discoloured after just one meal, and all of it got discoloured when not being used so it was a major job to clean before guests came. It meant double the amount of ware in the kitchen on The Night. And it was often three or four days before all the 'best' entertaining items were back in their cabinets.'

Anna and Don bought pretty nice stainless steel cutlery which they use every day. And crockery from an open pattern. That way, they were able to buy as few or as many of each item as they wanted, including spares. This is also used every day.

'Our menus rely on dishes that we cook fairly frequently, so there's no panic or uncertainty about them. And often guests will bring a desert or a salad. In the past twelve months we have had terrific evenings like this several times and I know that our feeling of relaxation conveys itself to our guests. We're no longer behind in our invitations – we may even be in that dreaded category that people feel they owe us!'

'Living in the country, we insist on "indoor slippers",' says **Paula**. 'As a child I remember envying families with that as a house rule. It seemed cosy and ordered and secure.

'Now that we have a young family it has really practical

advantages for us. Dirt is not dragged through the home, and it's quieter.

'My children accept the rule with no problem,' she says. 'We've been doing it since they were little, so we all do it automatically now – my husband and I included, of course.'

'When choosing colour schemes, we've sometimes seen friends put down pale carpets or buy a pale-coloured sofa and chairs,' says **Bríd**. 'With young children, our home decor approach has to be more practical.

'If we want to use light colours, we'll use them on the easier-to-clean surfaces such as washable walls or curtains, but not carpets. We usually look for camouflage colour for carpets or soft furnishings. This means a pattern but it doesn't have to be gaudy – a subtle two-tone will do the trick. And if fabrics have been treated during manu- facture with a "Scotchguard" type of stain repellent, they are easier to keep clean.

'Is something stains, prompt treatment may save the day. Cold water, dabbed on and sponged off, is a good first-aid for most stains. Proprietary stain removers come with instructions.

'Protection! Loose covers or even loose "armlets" for easy chairs will make it easier to keep the furniture clean. Similarly, padded mattress protectors, and all-over matt- ress covers under the sheets are well worthwhile. And pillow protectors under pillow covers.

'Our last advice is about stair carpet. If you buy it longer than required you can move it slightly up or down (and you *should* move it up or down) every six months or so. This spreads the wear and helps prevent bald patches.

'Rooms have personalities. And they can have behaviour problems too!' say **Ciara and Ron**.

'The more multi-purpose a room, the harder it is to get right. A room that has to accommodate TV/radio, books and magazines, toys, hobbies, clothes, eating, sleeping, is difficult to organise. We've all known rooms that seemed impossible to manage, that looked a mess after half an hour. Our children's bedrooms were like that. Then we realised that it wasn't the children's fault, it was the room set-up that made it difficult to manage.

'So we gave serious thought to organising and planning for all the bedroom activities and spent some money on it. We got storage that the children could reach and manage themselves, and it has been a great success. It had been so discouraging when the rooms were difficult to keep.'

An easy-to-manage room is one that has its personality and purpose clear: what it's intended for, what activities take place there, what's stored there.

'If I were shipwrecked on a desert island, the luxury I would like is a microwave oven,' says **Áine**. 'Some people use theirs only for defrosting food from the freezer, and it is great for that. But they miss out on a lot. When we first got ours we spent a few evenings trying out some "real" meals, and we wouldn't be without it now.'

'Some microwaves are more versatile than others. We asked friends what kind they had and what they cooked in them. And devoted an evening or two to getting the most out of it. It cuts down on dirty saucepans – you can cook, serve and even eat from the same dish. It's also great for latecomers, who can quickly heat up their own meal.'

'My quick convenient food wizard is a timer on our oven,' says **Larry**. 'When we come home in the evening there's no waiting, no fussing. A casserole and potatos were popped into the oven in the morning; the oven switched itself on in the afternoon. It's piping hot, ready to eat, and the smell in the kitchen is wonderful to come home to.'

June works in a restaurant so she knows that specials of any kind take extra time and effort.

'At home we had non-standard china and glassware. It was very nice, mostly things that we had been given as gifts,' she says. 'But it needed special attention: some items were more fragile than the rest, some of it didn't stack in our presses. But homes don't have room for stray or random items unless they are really special. For one thing, they don't pay their way because they need special attention, aren't that versatile, take up more room. In the end we went out and bought lots of the same product and it has certainly made life easier.'

Start your simplification in the shop at purchasing time, by buying items that are easy-care, and that are identifiable-per-person (so that individuals can take responsibility for their upkeep).

You can break these rules if you find something that you really adore!

4
How to: Tidy and Clean

A frisk, a booster, a blitz

Housework comes in three thoroughnesses: a frisk, a booster and a blitz. A daily frisk will keep things going OK provided that a more thorough job, a booster, is done one to three times during the week.

However homes also need more than that periodically. In-depth cleaning and reorganisation will reach those parts not reached during the daily and weekly rush. That's a blitz.

That is the rhythm of housework: frisk, booster, blitz.

Tidy and clean

Tidy is not the same as clean. People notice tidy or untidy – they don't notice clean or dirty to the same extent. That's good, because a place can be tidied in minutes. A five-minute frisk makes a big impression on tidiness. Cleaning takes longer and it's not worth doing unless things are tidy first.

Every person needs to keep their own belongings tidy, all the time, every day. Only someone living in the home will know where things go – cleaning people will not know. The obvious person to tidy things away is the owner of the items.

No personal belongings scattered in communal areas is a good rule. Remember that if one person's belongings

are scattered or stuck in communal areas, it affects everyone else's use and enjoyment of the place. Communal areas are on loan to the entire household. They are not available for any individual to colonise.

Tidy up after each activity and tidy up especially last thing at night – a five-minute frisk will do it each time.

IF THINGS ARE LEFT LYING AROUND?

Homes need a tidy-up container or two, perhaps one upstairs, one downstairs. This can be a shelf or drawer or box so long as it is a designated and known place to chuck out-of-place belongings on a daily basis. The owners can retrieve them from the container. But you may have to take action if they are left lying around too often, or for too long.

Shane tried the confiscating method. 'I never thought I would be able to hide a favourite plaything or garment,' says Shane. 'But when I did it as a last resort, it worked. I had to do it only once or twice. Then everyone realised that the rule was here to stay.'

Barbara had a variation on that. 'I was tired of finding cups and snack items beside the chairs, on the living room floor. I wanted to find a way to make the point without scolding or nagging. So one day last week I gathered up the crisp packets and the comics and the cup. I put them in a plastic bag, under my daughter's duvet. It did the trick. She got the message!'

WHERE TO START?

Before starting, be clear about where you are going to finish. Finish with the cleaning items and vacuum back in place, cleaning cloths and mop washed and hung to dry,

HOME CLEANING SPECIAL OFFER

Home-cleaning firms estimate three to four hours to clean a two- to three-bedroom home. This is booster cleaning; it's not like blitz cleaning. It does not include picking up your belongings; your place has to be surface-tidy before the start. This special offer includes no thinking or deciding but it's good value all the same for three hours' work. It doesn't all have to be done by one person or at one time. Reckon on 20–30 minutes per room.

What it includes:

- Removing room's non-belongings: newspapers, cups, plates
- Bagging the garbage
- Tidying what belongs in the room
- Grooming behind the cushions, behind furniture. Lifting cushions, moving furniture on castors, paying attention to corners, edges of floors or surfaces
- Damp-dusting or dry-dusting the hard surfaces: tables,shelves, fingermarks on doors and light switches, TV screen and TV. Lifting objects and ornaments in order to do so
- Floors: vacuum or brush and damp-mop, including corners

and a clean and tidy 'look' on the place. And the garbage out in the garbage spot.

Do you start at the same place on each occasion so that some places will never get done? Start with the easiest and cleanest? Or the hardest and dirtiest? It depends on which will give you more encouragement to continue. Start at the top and work down, or start at the bottom and work up? Start at the livingroom and work clockwise? If there is time to do the entire home, it doesn't matter which room you start at. But if somewhere will be left out, start at a different place on each cleaning day. If you always start at the same spot, but never finish, the same spots will be left unfinished each time.

Most homes have a busy 'core' area that needs boosting every cleaning day (the living room, hall, stairs, bathroom(s), kitchen, laundry area). Less used rooms such as bedrooms are then cleaned less frequently, in rotation – a different area each time.

Top priority is keeping the hall looking good, every day. To do this needs disciplined management and cooperation from everyone. Remember: don't centralise belongings in the hall; decentralise them to the bedrooms.

BATHROOMS

There is more to cleaning a bathroom than squirting a strong-smelling cleanser into the toilet pan and opening the window. These tiny rooms can take as long to clean as a living room.

A toilet pan is constructed so that splashes don't bounce out. Most splashes are caught by the fold-down of the porcelain rim. Toilet cleanser needs to be squirted into the underside of the fold and it will then drain into the pan. These cleansers are slow acting and it is recommended that they be left on overnight.

Water contains mineral deposits, tiny solids that can build up in the part of the toilet pan that is filled with water, especially in hard water areas. Overnight cleanser, together with regular daily brushing with a toilet brush can prevent the buildup. Deposits also remain when water or urine evaporates. Splashes on the toilet seat or wall will dry to leave browny stains and discolouration. These are difficult to remove if left to harden, particularly near the hinge parts of toilet seats. Abrasive cleansers will only scratch the seat and make the next cleaning more difficult. Try a non-abrasive cleanser. Do this frequently to avoid build-up. Frequency, preventing build-up, is all-important. The problem is usually that you don't notice these stains until they have hardened. If they get unpleasant looking, it is possible to buy replacement hinges for most toilet seats. Or you could replace the seat altogether.

On cleaning day, damp wipe the outside of the pedestal to the floor and the plumbing bends; damp wipe or clean the seat, especially where the hinges attach it to the pan; brush the inside of the pan; clean the adjacent walls where splashes and discolouration can build up.

Shower cubicles also get hard water and soapy build-up and need non-abrasive cleanser to clean them, as do washbasins and baths.

Body hair is towelled on to the bathroom floor. If it's a hard floor, damp wipe it with tissue before washing. Using discardable tissue means that hairs, fluff and nail clippings are not recirculated. Vacuum carpeted floors.

Clean mirrors at least once a week as splash marks are very noticeable.

Tiling grout is a bathroom weak spot. It is difficult to clean and shows dirt and damp stains. Clean it with a brush and non-abrasive cleanser, or a special purpose grout cleanser.

Try not to leave cleaning items standing on the floor where each item has to be lifted when cleaning the floor. Ideally keep them in a ventilated bathroom cupboard where damp cloths can be hung up to dry, ready for next use. The bathroom cleaning kit consists of:

- waste bin
- two cleansers is enough. One for WC bowl, one all-purpose cleanser for everything else
- WC brush in its container
- brush for nooks and crevices, mild scouring pad, wipes, tissues, disposable cloths

PERIODIC BLITZES

Special cleaning of soft and hard surfaces and light fixtures, reorganising drawers and closets and throwing stuff out used to be called spring cleaning.

But how frequently? If you were an hotel or super-market, you would have wall charts of timetables for how frequently the different periodic chores had to be done. In your home, it may be like with gardening: you keep an eye on the hedge and you trim it within a week or two of noticing it needs to be done. Perhaps you can go an extra three weeks before cutting it, if it has not been fast-growth weather. Perhaps it needs doing more frequently in summer. It's kind of a 'taste it and see' timetable, and the time for tasks like this probably comes out of time that would otherwise be recreation.

Don't start a blitz without the time to finish it, or to finish the portion you start. And be determined to get rid of the resulting discards.

Do tidy a room drawer by drawer, closet by closet, not all in one grand splurge. To be over-ambitious and empty the entire contents of a room into the middle of a floor is asking for trouble. You are risking not having the time to finish it. Then it will become necessary to bundle everything higgledy piggledy out of the way. It's essential to start only the portion that you can finish that day. A half-finished job is fine – as long as you've planned it to be half-finished. A job that is accidentally half-finished is bad news. When you pick it up again you have to backtrack.

And don't clear or clean one room by chucking everything into another room!

5
How to: Meals

Deciding

So you like the fun of deciding on something at the last moment? Save that fun for outings, meetings, non-urgent stuff. It's not for meals. Meals will take least time if they are thought about in advance. Hesitation and uncertainty could add half-an-hour a day to meal preparation. And the nearer to mealtime you leave it, the more hassle it is.

If you're at home during the day, decide on the day's main meal at breakfast. If you go out to work, the evening meal should preferably be decided on the night before, certainly before you leave in the morning. That's each day's meal on a day-to-day basis, but chosen from a week's advance planning and purchases.

Shopping

If you do a main shopping once a week, plan a week's menus in advance. If you do a main shopping once a month, plan a month's menus.

After you've been doing it for several months, you will know your household's eight or ten OK menus. With children you may have only two or three OK menus! And you will know what to purchase for them. Until then it's a good idea to jot down the days ahead and a meal for each day. List any special ingredients, and any last-minute

To make toast: first you burn it;
then you scrape it.

fresh purchases required nearer the day. Your home's food storage capacity will influence how many days' meals you can stock. Certainly a week, if you have a fridge and freezer.

But watch out on shopping days. Putting away a supermarket shop in the kitchen will take half- to three-quarters of an hour. In addition, putting food away in the freezer could take an extra half-hour's preparation – portioning, wrapping, part-cooking. So don't overbuy or you may fail to deal with all the food at its best. If you can feed your purchases on to the supermarket conveyer belt with all similar items together, your at-home unpacking should be much easier.

Meat from the supermarket will not keep long, even in a refrigerator, if wrapped in clingfilm. The clingfilm seems to make it sweat and deteriorate more rapidly. It needs to be unwrapped and stored on loosely covered plates or containers. And clingfilm is not thick enough to prevent freezer burn in freezers.

It's worthwhile drafting a master shopping list. List your home's usual purchases (brands, sizes) in the order of their layout in your usual supermarket. Leave space at the bottom of the list for additional items, and make photocopies of the list. It will be very useful if others are doing the shopping – it will save them buying Brand X instead of Brand Y. It's useful also to keep a weekly copy posted in the kitchen. Everybody notes what is running short, what's needed. So the shopping list is practically ready on shopping day.

TIME THE COOKING TO SUIT THE COOK

The day you bring home the shopping, try to leave some time for cooking or part-preparation of purchases. I buy six pounds of mincemeat and casserole it with onions and vegetables (in two pots as I have none big enough for six pounds). It can be shaped in meatballs. Or you could choose beef pieces or chicken pieces instead. Next morning I skim off any fat and bag it into meal-sized portions. I cannot tell you how welcome those portions are in the following weeks. Five minutes in the morning will ensure that you come home in the evening to delicious dinner-ready smells. In the morning five minutes you unwrap and put the frozen cooked food into a covered oven dish. Scrub potatoes and pierce the skins in two or three places with a knife or fork in order to allow steam to escape. Put everything in the oven and time the oven to cook for one hour. The basic cooked mincemeat can have curry sauce added, or tomato sauce to make a bolognese. That's timing the cooking to suit the cook.

TIPS FOR EFFICIENCY

- Start from a clear working area so that you don't have to press less suitable areas into use. This will cause a headache at clearing-up time.
- Clear up as you go. Clear after each stage, leaving a minimum of debris at the end.
- Peel vegetables on to a newspaper that is then tidily bundled into the garbage.
- Ask for a helper to stand by ten minutes before mealtime to set the table and help clear the preparations before eating.

- Latecomers should expect to serve themselves, and not expect the cook to hang around or to delay their own eating. Latecomers should also clear away after themselves.

TIME THE SERVING TO SUIT THE EATERS

At present my children are on serious study routines. We have agreed a six o'clock evening mealtime. By deciding and starting the ball rolling at breakfast time, I manage to come very close to target. If the meal is much delayed I know that it really throws their timetables.

Having meals ready on time is one of the most difficult things for beginners. Three or more items which require different cooking times and methods, all to be ready at the same time? There are two good solutions:

- Plan to have the meal ready ten to fifteen minutes ahead, to be kept hot until mealtime. Ovenproof dishes in the oven are fine. Then, if the timetable slips a bit, you have a safety margin. Roast joints of meat actually *require* to be out of the oven twenty minutes before being carved, in order to set.
- Much of the preparation can be done up to twenty-four hours in advance, leaving the actual meal in a timed oven to switch on and cook by itself, to be ready at homecoming. Perhaps do a half-hour preparation the previous evening or in the morning and either leave the food to cook on a timer or spend a half-hour cooking it just before the meal.

Setting the table can cause a last- minute delay. If I haven't a ten-minute helper before the meal, I set the table early in the course of preparation (if not in the morning).

TIME THE CLEAR-AWAY TO SUIT CLEARERS-AWAY

You make the meal, you eat the meal, you clear up after the meal. Right? Wrong. Make the meal, clear up most of the preparation, then eat the meal. In this way, the final clear-away will be as short as possible. The meal cooked, ready and keeping hot ten to fifteen minutes before eating has a great side-effect. It leaves time for most, if not all of the clearing away to be done before the meal is served: counters and cooker cleaned, pots washed and put away or put into the dishwasher. The result is a minimum to be done afterwards. Clearing-up help is often more readily available before a meal than afterwards, especially if rostered.

It may mean thinking out some keep-hot techniques. And yes, additional serving dishes may be dirtied. Yes, you may miss the joyful spontaneity of platefuls straight from the skillet. But try it. Clearing after a meal is greatly eased if the preparation clutter is gone. It's greatly bogged-down if the preparation clutter is still there.

The evening meal clear-up is the loneliest job to do solo. Of all housework tasks, this is the one that begs for group effort. Households have got to have a shared system for it. OK, you try to have most of the clearance done before the meal, but it doesn't always happen that way. OK, so children may ask to leave the table early – but they need not escape clearaway duties. Everyone brings their own plate and things from the table, plus six items (or eight or five), so that the table is cleared. And everyone finishes the clear-up together, so that nobody is left doing a solo thirty-five-minute job. If washing-up is done in a bowl, prepare the bowl or assign somebody to prepare it before the meal begins: hot water, wash-up liquid. Everyone washes and dries their items, and puts them away.

Delay the coffee or tea until the main clearing is done. After all, at grand dinners people change location for coffee. This is precisely so as to permit the dinner table to be cleared and the washing-up to get underway.

6
HOW TO: LAUNDRY

The actual washing is not the problem. Clothes hanging around is the problem, waiting to be sorted (according to wash treatment), washed, dried, folded, ironed, sorted again (according to owner), put away. Many households with small children or a lot of members consider laundry to be the major workload, even ahead of meals.

There are two answers:

- Bring to the laundry area one washload at a time and one only. Pre-sort in the bedrooms.
- Better still, don't sort. Wash each person's belongings as a load – one load per person. OK, I know that sorted categories of load would wash more perfectly, all white things together, or all heavily soiled items together. But waiting for perhaps days while several different loads accumulate and become ready to wash is cumbersome. And studies show that most homes use only one or two wash programs no matter how many their machine offers. So one-person, one-wash load makes sense.

Especially if operated this way: the person who brings the one-person washload to the laundry area is the washload's owner. Yep. Everyone over the age of nine does their own wash. Over the age of twelve everyone changes their bed linen, washes and dries it and stores it back in their own

I COULDN'T FIND A CLEAN SHIRT TO IRON THIS
MORNING, SO I IRONED A DIRTY ONE.

bedroom ready for the next change.

If one person is doing all the laundry in a home with many children, there will probably be some washing every day – several daily laundry frisks. First of all you have to load the washing machine. Later on the items need to be taken out, hung, or folded or ironed. Or put aside for ironing later. Or the washing and the ironing could be done in lengthier once- or twice-a-week boosters.

HONEY, I SHRUNK THE WASHING. WHAT WENT WRONG?

Honey, the washing is shrunk, faded, colour-run, stretched, felted, still dirty, smelly, has electric static, is pilled, wrinkled, is torn, lost, has shredded tissue paper all over it. What went wrong?

Using the wrong washing machine program is the cause of most of these problems: water too hot; agitation too vigorous for the fabric; clothes left too long in the water; or left too long in a bundled-up damp condition; spin too long, tumble dry too hot.

Helpful instructions are available on detergent boxes, garment labels and in washing machine booklets. Follow them!

Some laundry hints:

- Don't let clothes get too dirty – they will not totally recover from it.
- Damp items become smelly if not hung to dry, for example if they are not removed from the washing machine promptly after washng, or if they are left bundled up damp in a laundry basket for days.
- Before washing, empty pockets, especially of tissues.

Otherwise shredded tissues get all over the wash.

- Before washing, turn inside-out those garments that might pick up fibres or fluff from other items.
- Before tumble-drying, untangle and shake out each garment individually. Make sure that nothing is bunched in difficult-to-dry folds.
- The iron's flat surface can develop a scorchy build-up. This has the habit of leaving brown marks on garments. Follow the iron manufacturer's instructions for cleaning the surface.
- Lost socks are the joke of every home, every washday. Buy three or four identical pairs, so as to be able to get a match, or put them in a pillowcase or 'smalls' bag before washing to keep them together.

A few laundry disasters seem to be necessary before people become competent, so don't be discouraged. It's a very good way to learn.

NEEDS OF THE LAUNDRY SET-UP

Not many homes have a dedicated laundry area. But aim for a clearly understood set-up. You want everyone doing their own laundry. That's why there must be nothing mickey mouse about its arrangements.

If the washing machine is in the kitchen, you may need to allocate time slots so as not to clash with whoever is using the cooker or sink. Perhaps designate a different day per person? Do not leave laundry in transit lying about the place and agree what to do when someone else's wash is already ahead in the system. Line-dry it? Hang it on coat-hangers, but where? Tumble-dry it? Leave it in a laundry basket? Yes, it takes a while to sort out the difficulties and misunderstandings that can arise when everyone is doing their own laundry. But it's definitely worthwhile, so don't give up.

In addition to the usual items, a laundry set-up needs:

- Discard bag. Don't-know and slow-lane items clutter the laundry area and the home. Put them into your discard bag. Then discard the contents. Don't hoard a full discard bag.
- Sewing items to sew on a button, mend a rip
- Hand washing possibility (bowl, hand-washing powder)
- Indoor line for drip dry and/or outdoor clothes line
- Storage for clean laundry, if possible near the laundry area.

THE LAUNDRY AREA DOES NOT NEED

spare parts for the grass cutter, old sports goods, toolbox items that have nothing to do with the laundry. Remove clutter and everything that doesn't belong.

FINISH THE LAUNDRY

Bob remembers a friend calling one day. 'He was horrified at the amount of washing I had to do,' says Bob. "But you just have so much laundry," he said. It was only after he had gone that I realised that he was looking at four stacked baskets full of clothes that had been there two or three weeks or more. I had just stopped noticing them. They were not urgent things, or they were only worn as a last resort. I had never got round to clearing them. When I did (including throwing a lot of the stuff out) it made the whole laundry area much easier to work in.'

7
HOW TO: CHILDCARE

There are plenty of helpful baby and childcare books and
magazines. They go into childcare in depth. Here I'll just
speak of a few household arrangements for children that
are sometimes overlooked.

WHERE IS YOUR BABY-CARE CENTRE, YOUR PLAY STORAGE?

A baby's bedroom, kitted out as the perfect nursery, needs
to be bonded with and cooperated with by parents.
Otherwise it can become a white elephant, little used
because somewhere else is more convenient or more
comfortable. Supplies and equipment may be stored in the
nursery but if another room is more comfortable, warmer
or handier, that's where the jobs will tend to get done.
As a result, equipment and supplies will be scattered,
difficult to locate. Will baby be bathed in the nursery or
in the bathroom? Or at the kitchen sink in a baby bath?
Will baby be dried and changed in the nursery (if it's
warm); or on your knee in the livingroom if the TV is there;
in the kitchen if you are supervising cooking; in your
bedroom if the cot is there; or at the telephone? It's worth
the effort of trying to stick to one supply depot only, and
being sure of finding the stuff there. If you need more
than one depot, equip more than one depot.

YOU NEVER ASK ME WHAT KIND OF A DAY
I'VE HAD AT HOME ALL DAY
SORRY DEAR. WHAT KIND OF A DAY HAVE
YOU HAD AT HOME ALL DAY?
DON'T ASK ME WHAT KIND OF A DAY
I'VE HAD AT HOME ALL DAY

When your child is bigger, the nursery may not be where your child wants to play. In front of the TV, or in the kitchen where there's company may be the preferred place. In that case, will you store toys in the livingroom or kitchen, or will you make a tidy-up rule that each day things go back to storage in the bedroom? A small toybox in the livingroom, the rest in the bedroom? If your children have too many toys, withdraw some from circulation for a few weeks. They'll get more fun from them when they're fresh again. Perhaps have a different-coloured toy box per child? Or per type of toy? A playmat – a cloth on which toys are restricted in a nice way – is good. It means 'this is my toy patch'.

AT HOME ALL DAY WITH CHILDREN

Caring for a newborn baby can take all day. While baby sleeps, you try to catch up on your sleep and on the housework. While baby is awake you will be getting to know and enjoy one another. And all the time baby's wakefulness, need of company, cuddling, stimulation and food will be changing. You will be trying to adapt and respond to these changes and you will also be adjusting your home to the changing demands of a growing and exploring child. A baby is like the seven dwarfs: grumpy dozy, sleepy, happy – and all the rest rolled into one.

Caring for a baby affects the time you have left to do the housework and get on with other aspects of your life – there is less of it. You stay in your dressing-gown and pick things up and put them down without doing anything about them.

If you are getting only the bare minimum of housework

done, let it be your opportunistic clear-it-yourself, clean-it-yourself tasks and every day's six essential tasks. As children get bigger, build tidy-up time into your activities and theirs. Five minutes before an activity ends and five minutes before bedtime is sufficient. This is the start of yellow belt habits that will be a satisfaction to them and to you in the short, medium and long term. Help them to hang up and care for their own things.

Get the housework done and mind children at the same time? I never found it possible to concentrate on serious housework when young children were up and round about. Being on call for their queries or problems, being alert to their needs, being interrupted, all these bring housework to a slowdown or a stop. And any helpers I have had in my home majored in either one or the other. Either they were great at cleaning and less good with kids; or not so good at cleaning but my kids felt very happy with them.

CHILDREN AND YOU ARE OUT DURING THE DAY

Having dinner ready as you come home in the evening is the best help. You don't have to fuss in the kitchen but can devote time to the children. Ten minutes then will reassure and cosset children more than thirty minutes later on.

Why have two experts on babycare, cookery? If Mom is home all day with the baby (or toddlers) it seems sensible for her to do all the housework as well? Of course the answer is that every enterprise needs versatile people who can tackle every job. Children need both parents. And a home doesn't have room for specialists who can only tackle one job. Everyone needs to be able to tackle all of your home's tasks.

Rushed times

The morning rush, the evening rush, the bedtime rush.

Getting up: Give every child their own alarm clock. Clothes should be laid out the night before. Your tidy-up times during the day and before bedtime will help.

Clothes

Not too many, not too few: Five or six sets for younger children who may need two changes a day, three or four sets after about age five. The quicker they can be washed and back in circulation, the fewer you need.

Quality time and quantity time

Caring for children does not divide neatly into quality time and quantity time. You can make loving and nurturing time out of everyday care routines such as feeding and changing baby and getting on with the housework.

A hands-on parent who provides everyday care and company will benefit from this contact, and so will the child. It's a great conduit for communication, especially as children get older.

Childcare can take from twenty hours a week to twenty hours a day, depending largely on the age of your child or children. Parents should share the housework because it's the only decent thing to do and share childcare because it's good for you and for your children.

In a European Union document an interesting distinction is made on housework-sharing patterns among adults. Many fathers dressed their children in the morning. But choosing what the child would wear was a separate undertaking.

Fathers, go the extra mile. Choose what your child will wear. This will mean knowing what's clean and what your child enjoys wearing. It will mean washing the clothes often enough to have supplies of the appropriate warmth always available. Perhaps you need to buy extra garments? (Then go the extra two miles!)

Childcare edges into every aspect of your work and social and home life, on top of, between, around and instead of existing activities. Let's be parent-centred for a moment. Perhaps limit children's floor area (no toys in the livingroom), or limit their time there (no toys in the livingroom after six pm)? Preserve a spot for yourself so that you can find your things where you left them, not broken or scattered. Plan personal time and space for yourself.

8
How to Stop Worrying and Love Entertaining

Decide your best entertaining plan and equip for it

There are hundreds of good ways to entertain but you don't need hundreds. Settle for one or at most two that suit your way of thinking, your home, your budget and the time you have available. Settle and decide on one at your leisure. Then equip for it, perfect it, and roll it into action when needed. On each occasion that you entertain, you do not want to be wondering which of the hundreds of ways to do it this time. You want to be activating your known plan, using your established equipment, having no last-minute uncertainties or panic.

Not all entertaining occasions are identical. But most occasions can be adapted to your one or two chosen formulas. You can depend on these to establish a warm, in-control atmosphere. This is much easier than trying to organise a new formula each time.

Once you iron out the wrinkles in your plan your guests will experience a welcoming reassuring feeling when they visit your home. This will allow you to vary or to take it a bit easier with the last-minute things.

No, a plan will not ruin the spontaneity of your event.

It will provide the dependable backdrop for the day's fun, and can be used over months and years of entertaining.

Perhaps choose one for a small number, one for a larger number; or one for an informal event and one for a posh event; one with food, one without. Perhaps you will decide that fork suppers for twenty are not your scene or your home's scene; that a supper for six or for eight is better. If you do a good once-off job of equipping for one or two chosen entertaining formulas, it is half the battle for ever more.

Work out the finer details in advance. Where will you put guests' coats? Will they take them there themselves? How will they retrieve them? How and where to serve drinks? Do you have ice-containers, ice-making trays or bags? Does any furniture or lighting need to be moved? Or borrowed or bought? If you are serving food, what kind can you manage? Have you enough crockery and cutlery for what you plan? Do you need to hire anything and from where?

Clean table cloth? Coathangers for twelve? Ice bucket(s)? They've been ready and waiting for weeks and months so there's no last minute panic about them. Designate a 'guest chest' where items for guest entertaining are stored and available. Include clean aprons and dishcloths. When guests are coming it's not the time for grubby everyday aprons.

What is the best way to issue invitations? Do you issue invitations as a spur to tidy your home? Be sure to tell your guests what you'll be serving (i.e. a sandwich or a three-course meal), and who will be coming.

On each occasion decide in advance what you will be

wearing. And as for the children: prepare clean pyjamas; perhaps move the TV to their bedroom. Organise a minder for them? Or ask can they stay at a friend's home?

THE PLAN

Owning nice tableware and serving dishes isn't enough. Easy access to them, superlatively easy access, both for taking out beforehand and, equally important, for putting away afterwards, is essential.

This suggests an idea that makes more and more sense the more you think about it. Everyday cookware and tableware is best. It's close to hand and you're used to it. And it means that your kitchen will not have to accommodate two sets on the night – everyday and good ware. Best of all, the aftermath will not take several days to give special cleaning treatment to and put away. Guest tableware can take up a lot of room, grow musty-smelling between uses, and may require hand washing and silver polishing before and after using it.

Buy your everyday table ware from an 'open' pattern. That is, it's possible to buy individual pieces – eight plates, sixteen cups – to allow for breakages. Cups seem to break more readily than anything else. Buy plenty of ware. Then when guests are coming, it's just like an ordinary table setting. 'Everyday +' would mean adding a special touch to your table – flowers or candles, or a dainty tablecloth.

Everyday food is best also. Think simple. It does not have to be a meal. A drink, a coffee, can be as enjoyable as a full meal. Back to your place for soup after the match, or a weekend brunch? Or a bring-your-own beer session with you providing the sandwiches.

Start at the bottom of the scale of difficulty and trade up if you wish. That's better than starting at the top and feeling that you're trading down.

The entertaining quandary is how to go to enough trouble to convince guests they're welcome without going to so much that they think they're too much trouble and you are exhausted. Effortless it must appear. That's easiest done if it *is* effortless or relatively so.

Guests love the informality of no-hype entertaining. Big-hype entertainers seldom get invited back because nobody feels adequate to match their standards.

If you can practise and perfect a nice everyday dinner and then ask guests to it on a future occasion, you'll do that best. Don't attempt an untried menu. And don't plan more than one hot course. Perhaps a guest could bring a salad or desert. Alternatively, buy ready prepared food from a delicatessen or home-cook shop.

Get to know how long things take. Maybe fifteen minutes to set a table or one hour to set out a buffet table. Or twenty minutes to carve in the kitchen and plate in the kitchen hot food for eight people.

How will you serve food for a sit-down meal? Plated in the kitchen? Filled serving dishes brought to table for each diner to self-serve from, or for one diner to serve the others' plates? Attempt 'silver service' only if you have serving help; that is, diners' empty plates are served from people's left-hand side and their plates are removed afterwards from their right-hand side.

Sleeping visitors? Spend a night sleeping in your guest bed to assess it. Supply a bedside light, tissues, reading material, spare blanket, spare pillow, hot water bottle, bowl of fruit, drinking water, towels.

MAKE IT CLEAR TO HELPERS WHAT HELP WILL BE NEEDED, WHEN

The trouble with cookery books is that they do not tell how, in addition to preparing delicious food, you can have your home clean, bathroom tidy, children quiet and yourself looking spick and span – and all by 7.30 for 8 pm! The day before is never long enough to get everything done the day before.

If you can get help, do so! Most friends are flattered to be asked to help, and they know that it means you would be prepared to do the same for them on a later occasion. Your helpers and your family need to be ready at least a half-hour beforehand. That's so that they will:

- not have grooming preoccupations when you need their help
- not need the bathroom when you do, and not be using it right after it has got its polish and sparkle for guests
- not need to use the telephone when you need their help
- not need your help just when you need theirs (can you find my brown shoes, iron my shirt?)
- answer and greet early guests, take coats, chat to them to create that buzz of fun and companionship and stop you feeling panic before the first guests arrive
- be ready for a final briefing about the scenario. What will be happening when? What assistance is required?

You should have outlined this to your helpers hours or days beforehand. The crucial understanding to achieve is this. Are they to:

a) undertake a specific task or tasks?

or

b) stand by, ready to follow your instructions when you issue them?

or

c) use their own initiative to mingle, pass food, see what's to be done and do it?

I've held parties where we hadn't established this. And I would say to a helper: 'Please serve coffee to the group near the window' and receive the reply: 'I can't, I'm washing these plates/eating this sandwich/fixing this flower arrangement.' Of course I wasn't giving good instructions. You need to clear with your helpers how you'll operate and communicate. For clearing away afterwards, decide whether you're happy for washing-up to be going on while party guests are still there? Will you encourage everyone to help with clearing away before home time?

Specific tasks to allocate to helpers are:

* drinks organiser and server
* door opener/greeter and coat taker
* conversation starter
* last-minute inspector of the loo (tidy? soap? paper? clean towel?)
* table setter before, putter-away of clean items afterwards. Help afterwards will be much more effective if the putter-away has seen where things come from and are stored.
* desert: produce/display/serve

- coffee: beforehand, set out cups, sugar/cream and coffee maker; make and serve the coffee or tea. This is a great help as the host or hostess is usually pretty tired at this stage and has possibly been bustling a bit. Being able to stop bustling while someone else takes over will be a relief to everyone.
- entertain/mind the children

Does everyone in your home understand that the place needs to be clean and kept tidy, and coat hooks emptied not just five minutes before guests arrive, but a day or two before?

Happy entertaining!

TIME AND MOTION STUDY ASKS:
WHY AM I STANDING HERE AT MIDNIGHT SPENDING
TEN MINUTES IRONING THIS SHIRT?

9
TIME AND MOTION STUDY AND HOUSEWORK

Time and motion study asks Why? Who? How? Where? When? How long?

Why am I standing here at midnight spending ten minutes ironing this shirt?

- *Why:* iron? (Could it drip-dry?)
- *Who:* me? (Who else could do it?)
- *How:* standing? (Is there a better method?)
- *Where:* here? (A more efficient or comfortable place?)
- *When:* at midnight? (A more convenient time?)
- *How long:* ten minutes? (Is there a quicker way to do it?)

You may have a gut feeling that a task doesn't need to be done at all. Or that someone else should do it. Or that it could be done differently, elsewhere, at a more convenient time or more quickly.

Time and motion study lets you get in touch with these gut-feelings systematically. It may even throw up new gut-feelings! It looks at every bit of every task to see: does it need to be done? Does it need to be done by this person, in this way, in this place, at this time, for this duration?

How time and motion study works

A comedienne once complained that she had 'been awake all last night for an hour'.

Without an accurate picture of which tasks are taking place or not taking place, and how and when, time and motion study cannot help. It obtains this accurate picture by observing and timing every bit of every task for a period. The trick is to be deadly accurate about what's going on when. And what's not going on. A lot of time is wasted in industry as in housework, by interruptions, searching for and fetching equipment, deciding what to do next, how to do it, and getting to the task's location. Experts will spot these dud or non-activities. Often workers do not realise how widespread they are until they are pointed out to them.

By studying the jobs you do, a time and motion expert can spot which tasks or portions of them are unnecessary. Or which could be done by a different person, in a different way, a different place, at a different time or more quickly.

Results can be dramatic: you do the same work in less time, or more work in the same time.

But housework is different from other jobs!

- Time and motion study is great for short repetitive tasks in industry. One minute saved on something that's repeated a hundred times a day results in a hundred minutes saved.

- But housework does not consist of the same task repeated a hundred times per day. It's a hundred different short tasks, needing to be done throughout the day, at different times of the day, and in different locations around your home.

- So to get the benefit of efficient methods in housework it's not just the time spent at each task that needs to be saved. Saving a minute off each of housework's many tasks is fine. But saving minutes before and after each task is almost more important.

- You achieve this by being opportunistic; do the task while you're on the spot – as the task arises. Everyone in the home should do the same. In that way, there is no time wasted getting back to the scene of the crime. And if it's done immediately it arises, there's no 'down' time during which the place looks grotty while the job is waiting to be done. The opportunistic task, done immediately on the spot by whoever gives rise to it, is a time and motion winner. Such tasks rarely take more than one to three minutes.

- It's not just the length of time a job takes that matters. It's when it's done that's important. Time-sensitive tasks need to be done as soon as possible so that the place looks good for the longest possible time. A fifteen-minute breakfast clear-away isn't as useful at seven in the evening as it would have been that morning straight after breakfast. Done in the morning it gives all-day benefit. Done in the evening it gives all-day glumness.

- However, booster and blitz tasks are not as time-sensitive as CIY and every day's six tasks. Being able to choose your time to do booster and blitz is a great help to efficiency and to feeling in control.

- In industry, it's efficient to do similar-type work in bulk. All item A is done one week; all item B the next week. This doesn't suit homes or housework. Homes cannot stand the mess while a lot of chores accumulate. The exact opposite is what homes need: no accumulation, chores done as they arise. This leaves the place looking good for the longest time possible. In addition, large blocks of time for bulk housework are hard to come by. Small fragments of time are easier to find, five minutes or so at a time.

- Frank Gilbreth, author of *Cheaper by the Dozen*, always buttoned his shirt from bottom to top, because he found he could do it in seven seconds from bottom to top, whereas it took nine seconds from top to bottom. Looked at one way, this is a saving of almost 25 per cent of time. But looked at another way, the saving amounts to only fourteen seconds per week. So don't be dazzled by time and motion study. Taking out the vacuum to do just one room may add three minutes to the job. But if it gets it done at a time that suits you, that's efficiency. A bulk approach can be useful for out-of-home tasks. Do all your out-of-home chores in one trip – shopping, shoe repairs, dry cleaning, library. But a bulk approach isn't beneficial for all housework tasks.

- Housework is different also because homes are for fun as well as for housework. Housework tasks can be speeded up by efficiency. The nurturing and fun things in a home cannot. Speeding up the washing-up time is not the same as speeding up cuddle-time. Often there's a conflict between doing a good job at the housework and doing a good job at nurturing, caring and fun. Efficiency isn't the only goal in homes.

- Housework needs to be worker-friendly. In your home, you are sometimes the worker, sometimes the user of that work. Make life easy for when you are doing the work. Store clean dishes near where they are washed, not in a remoter area near the dining table. Store clean laundry in the laundry area so that the laundry work will be finished quicker by getting rid of the added laundry burden of delivering things to several different storage spots. Let the users come and fetch their supplies, rather than expecting the laundry person to deliver them.

WHAT IS A ROUTINE?

Time taken on jobs breaks down into:

- warming-up time
- actual job time
- cooling-down time

If you cut out everything except 'actual job' time, you can get through work a lot more quickly. A routine helps you to do this. A bunch of jobs that you do one after the other at the same time of the day or week – that's a routine.

However exciting your life is, housework remains the same. The same jobs recur at the same time intervals and need to be done within the same time-scale. The best time solutions for one day or one week are likely to be the best for every day and every week.

That is what most people mean when they speak of a routine for housework. The best time solutions of previous days and weeks are used day after day and week after week.

A routine is an efficient use of time. It is a seven-day overview of what needs to be done in the home, and the best time-slot for each. And a commitment to that time slot.

The commitment is worthwhile because it results in maximum work for minimum effort. There's no indecision or wondering or foostering for supplies. You could spend as much energy and time at sizing up jobs and trying to avoid doing them as the jobs themselves would consume. If you have to stop and think what you're going to do, you often do nothing. Having supplies to hand, knowing what job comes next and getting on with it – all these help you to use time efficiently.

HOUSEWORK ROUTINES
- Every day's six tasks
- Every week's boosters. These need doing one to three times a week.
- Periodic blitzes. These need doing from one to twelve times a year.

EVERY DAY'S SIX TASKS

There are only six or so timetabled tasks that have to be done every day. One or one-and-a-half hours could get them all done. You know for certain that this bunch of jobs will crop up each day come rain, come shine. That's in addition to everyone in the home doing their clear-it-yourself, clean-it-yourself tasks throughout the day, throughout the home.

1 Prepare main meal.
2 Meal clear-up. No solo clear-ups after communal meals.
3 A thorough kitchen job at least once a day. There's no point trying to pretend that it's not needed. Individual CIY still leaves an overall kitchen task to be done: including emptying the garbage and sweeping or washing the floor.
4 Frisk livingroom and hall.
5 Any other tasks special to your home – tend the furnace, deal with the cat litter, ten or fifteen minutes laundry. Of course if you have baby and child care, it is an occupation in itself. It can occupy an elastic amount of time. It will have its own every day's six-or-more tasks, as well as its boosters and perhaps blitzes. That's in addition to the housekeeping chores.
6 A share of the week's boosters or periodic blitzes.

Identify these tasks as those that must be done every day if your home is to manage. But if the time is spent on other jobs, no matter how many daffodils have been planted or curtains made or windows cleaned, the place will be sloppy for the day.

Target for as many as possible of every day's six tasks to be done first thing in the morning. Nobody should go out in the morning before playing his or her part.

You know the saying: 'An hour's sleep before midnight is worth two hours after midnight'? Well, an hour's housework before midday is worth two hours after midday. The later in the day chores are left, the less time there is to do them, and the harder they are to face. The breakfast table straight after breakfast is OK, but six hours later it's dismaying. If it's going to be done sooner or later, the sooner it's finished, the longer your home will look nice.

If that is all you can manage on most days, that's OK. But on some days of the week, perhaps at the weekend or evenings, it will be time to catch up on every week's tasks and on periodic tasks.

EVERY WEEK'S BOOSTERS

Not all your home needs to be or can be done every day. Many tasks need attention one to three times a week. These will probably total from ten to thirty hours of housework a week. Many people do a bit each day on most days, in addition to that day's six. Or people do only the six from Monday to Friday and tackle the boosters on Saturday.

Every week's booster tasks are:

- Tidying and cleaning 'boosters'
- Food planning, preparation and shopping
- Laundry

How frequently? It's a matter of trial and error, depending on how high your standards and your energy are, the time you and your household members are making available for housework, the space and facilities in your home.

Is it necessary to roster specific times? For once-a-week chores lasting a half-hour or more, it is worth keeping a weekly appointment in mind, whether the job will be done by a purple or black belt. Lengthy stretches of time do not fall off the back of a lorry; you cannot grab them opportunistically. If you commit to the same time of the week each week, it should bring at least three benefits. First, the task will not be forgotten. Second, the remainder of the week will be free of such tasks. Third, you may be able to depend on a helper if you commit to a time and get a helper to commit also. A supermarket shopping trip will be eased if helpers are at home to help unload and put away purchases. If you shop opportunistically you may have to unload on your own.

Although you might think that once every five or nine days would be the best frequency for some tasks, try to fit them into a seven-day pattern. Vacuuming the hall and livingroom once a week whether they need it or not may seem a waste. Elizabethans used to bath once a year whether they needed it or not. But regularly updated housework is not a waste. It prolongs the OK condition of the home, extends it until the next scheduled attention. And it helps to prevent your having to give emergency unscheduled attention at awkward moments.

When life is so exciting that you do not know what you will be doing in an hour, or this evening, much less tomorrow or next Thursday, a routine for anything fights

ON ODD DAYS I LOOK AROUND THE HOUSE AND SEE
WHAT HAS TO BE DONE. AND I DO IT.
ON EVEN DAYS I LOOK AROUND AND I DON'T DO IT.

every instinct. But try it. It's OK if a task shifts from Wednesday to Thursday. But not if it shifts from Wednesday, period. 'On odd days I look around to see what has to be done and I do it. On even days I look around and I don't do it.' Once you get over the initial panic-despair mental shock or block about a routine per week it's easier, quicker and more efficient to get tasks done that way.

The thrill of living each day spontaneously and doing chores or not doing them according as you fancy, is not an efficient way to get housework done. By dealing with housework in a focused way you will get it done most quickly and most effectively. The saved time is then available to use as spontaneously as you wish.

PERIODIC OR 'BLITZ' TASKS

Periodic tasks aim to reach those parts that aren't reached during the every week rush. Periodic? It could be anything from once a month to once a year – or even less often. In homes you either schedule a time-slot each week for tackling different periodic tasks or you wait until you notice what needs doing and make time for it by cutting down on other activities. Not all periodic tasks are lengthy. Removing cobwebs from your entire home will take less than five minutes.

THE MACRO ROUTINE

A routine is really a budget of your time. It helps you to spend it at the time and in the way that is best for you, with the least waste.

With the macro routine, what matters are the blocks of time that are tied up, and at what times of the day – it's not all housework. A macro aims to give you a finish time as well as a start time.

- Early morning: one-and-a-half hours. I need one-and-a-half hours from alarm time in order to get everything done in a fuss-free fashion. This includes chores but also seeing the children off to school, eating my breakfast and looking after my personal grooming.

- Main meal time: one-and-a-half hours. One-and-a-half hours minimum from start to finish, with the washing-up done. That gives a half-hour to prepare, a half-hour to eat, a half-hour to clear away. So if we wish to be free in the evening at 7.30 we must start preparing the evening meal by six o'clock at the latest.

- Try a three-hour macro routine from five to eight in the evening. This could include meal prep-aration, eating, clearing away and wash-up, some of the week's tidy/clean or laundry, homework, baths, bedtime story or bedtime chat.

10
Time Management and Housework

The 90-minute hour

Never heard of it? Then you may have heard of the thirty-minute hour, where you achieve only half of the hour's possible work. In the ninety-minute hour you achieve much more than an hour's work.

The ninety-minute hour has no indecision, no 'attitude' problem, no interruptions.

No indecision about what you are going to do next. To get the best out of your time, you need to know what's waiting next in line to be done as soon as the present task is over. This overview of activities gives momentum, cuts out dawdling. It's the essence of a routine.

Indecision and hesitation waste time. For non-routine tasks, make a to-do list. In which order will you do these tasks? Number the items in this order. Preferably make the list the day before so that you hit the ground running the next morning. State your goal, not your activity. 'Tomorrow I'll prune the roses,' not 'Tomorrow I'll do some gardening'. Force results from yourself. It's not what you spend time at, it's what you get done that matters.

Routines are good largely because they cut out indecision. If you have to stop to think what to do next, you may just stop altogether.

You also need the job's requirements ready and waiting in the right spot – no hesitation while you search for tools or necessities.

No 'attitude' problem. You may be totally unsuited to housework. Your natural talents may be such that if you applied for the job you would not get it. But you did get it, and you may as well do it as quickly as possible. Everything will take twice as long if you sulk. Or if you worry. The task you dread, dislike or try to avoid will drag down your spirits until it's done. Do it.

No interruptions. Finish what you start. 'Business people waste one third of their time, on average. Interruptions are the main cause of wasted time'. This was written in a business publication about executives, but it applies to housework also. Don't interrupt yourself; don't let others interrupt you. Finish what you planned before moving on to something else. Interruptions mean broken concentration, scattered plans, having to start all over again.

If you are constantly being interrupted, try deliberately planning short stages. This makes it easier to complete a stage at a time without being interrupted before that stage is finished. The smaller the bites you take at jobs, the easier it is to complete those bites. A planned half-way house means breaking at a useful stage. An unplanned interruption means breaking at a bad place and having to backtrack, to start almost back at the beginning again.

Don't let others interrupt you. You can control some outside interruptions by, for example, not answering the telephone or doorbell, if you are stuck into an important job.

Children are constant interrupters. If you're in the middle of something, can you do a tender loving first aid, then finish your task before giving full-scale tender loving care.

In some kinds of work it can seem a good idea to leave part of a job undone, so that when you return to it, you are plunged straight back into it without delay or indecision. This tactic does not work well for housework. The satisfaction of a job completed, however short a job, is unbeatable, just as the dissatisfaction of a job not completed is disappointing. 'Close' jobs off; finish them.

LEISURE TIME

You don't want to give housework the best of your day. You want to save that for yourself. Nor the worst of your day as it will take twice as long when you're tired or dispirited.

If you always give to housework first choice of your day or week, you'll leave for yourself only fragments of free time that you cannot make much use of. Your leisure time will be sandwiched unsatisfactorily with your working time. Take the reverse approach. Fit housework into fragments of time. Housework doesn't mind. On the contrary, it prefers it. Doing bits and dabs of housework as you pass will keep the place looking good.

Avoid working anti-social hours, vacuuming at midnight, spending all weekend at the housework. Identify your prime times and claim them for yourself.

A typical problem arises in families at weekends. When everyone is at home, there is more work than on weekdays. Mothers often get caught in a trap of wanting to keep the family together and serve roast and three vegetables and make it enjoyable. That is a heavy chore. But it doesn't have to be an ambitious meal – an easy meal may be more fun. Perhaps if it has to be an ambitious meal it could be jointly prepared, making it into good family and visiting time. Or different family members could take it in turns to prepare. Don't make Sunday your hardest day.

'CRITICAL PATH' TIME MANAGEMENT – A SIMPLE IDEA

For the opening of its pets' corner next year, a zoo will need a baby lamb, a pony, a baby chimpanzee, a puppy, a baby elephant. The length of gestation time for these animals is as follows (longest first): elephant twenty-two months, pony eleven months, chimpanzee eight months, lamb five months, puppy two months. In order for all the baby animals to be ready at more or less the same time, the critical path for starting the pregnancies is:

- twenty-two months before opening: mother elephant
- eleven months before opening: mother horse
- eight months before opening: mother chimpanzee
- five months before opening: mother sheep
- two months before opening: mother dog

Don't start the puppies at the same time as the elephant, or the puppies will no longer be puppies by the time the baby elephant is born. And don't start the elephant last!

A critical path is useful in forward planning of all kinds. Whatever is going to take longest, start it first. Whatever will assist future chores, do it in time. Many home workers understand critical path planning, and use it without putting anything on paper. But for complicated or ambitious projects, it is worth writing down the various elements required and how long they will take and putting them into 'starting time' order. Typically, a Christmas dinner or other entertaining would benefit from a critical path timetable. It would be concerned with days or weeks ahead as well as minutes and hours on The Day. Even a laundry session uses this approach: if clean clothes are to be ironed on Wednesday evening, the wash has to be done several hours beforehand.

A formal critical path provides a countdown schedule for jobs, jobs that depend on an earlier section being completed before the next stage can go ahead. Or jobs that involve several elements of different duration.

Writing it down provides reminders for starting times or other critical stages, and helps to ensure that nothing is overlooked. Lots of jobs can be left to get on with it themselves, once they have been started in time.

'Our best critical path system is our dishwasher-emptying routine,' says Deirdre. 'Sean is first up in the morning and spends five minutes unloading the dishwasher then. It means that everyone can clear their breakfast things straight in to the dishwasher, wipe the table and put away whatever they have used – cereal, milk or bread.

'If Sean is away and the dishwasher isn't emptied, everyone leaves their things on the counter and nobody bothers to clear and wipe the table. The dishwasher has to be emptied eventually, but by then there's an additional four or five minutes work to deal with the accumulated dishes and the rest of the clearing.'

10–15 PER CENT COST OF LIVING

Don't expect to be 100 per cent productive 100 per cent of the time. If you have been trying to rush from activity to activity without pausing, pause.

Most activities require about 10 to 15 per cent of service time. This permits you to set up beforehand, tidy up afterwards, replenish supplies, keep your belongings organised. Surprise is inappropriate when a six-minute clear-up is required after a sixty-minute activity.

Business people in their work life, royalty and pop stars who have personal assistants can avoid spending this time. But Joe, Josephine and Josie Bloggs must personally assist themselves.

If you fail to anticipate this 15 per cent, you may often find that the spirit is willing but the timetable is unable.

11
ROSTERS

The mistake often made is to think you'll get action just by mentioning it once. Getting action requires repetition and reminders. And a roster for scheduled chores. No roster is needed for the non-scheduled, clear-it-yourself, clean-it-yourself chores. These are the one- to three-minute tasks that everyone gives rise to, done throughout the home throughout the day as they arise – by the person who causes them.

Marriage has been described as 'the deep calm of the double bed after the hurly-burly of the chaise longue'. Rosters offer the deep calm of anticipated task-doing after the hurly-burly of informal requests that are so often misunderstood, mistaken or missed.

Like a diet, people need to have thought through and 'bought' the idea of doing chores before they arise. So when it's time for action, there is no uncertainty. A roster provides this advance notice.

The same roster for eight weeks is best. A weekly changeover is too frequent. With a weekly change, neglected chores are always blamed on the other guy, and such a roster needs too much administration.

When you have a roster:

• Everyone sees that they are being asked a fair amount.

- When it is written down, arguments can be sorted out on paper in advance, not in the heat of the moment.
- The tasks should get done even if you're not there. You shouldn't have to nag for every two-minute chore.
- A roster saves excuses about forgetting, and Goodness, Sorry, Oops, No, Listen, I honestly didn't realise . . .
- Helpers get quick at, and bond with their chores.
- Everyone can plan their time better when they know what's expected of them.
- It's a good reminder for those who would never notice what has to be done.

On your roster you could have a section for every day's six (or so) jobs; plus a section for once- or twice-a-week boosters. Some tasks need quite precise timing. For others, a broader window of time is OK. Tidy/clean boosters between midday Thursday and midday Saturday could be a workable window: it would get the work done by an acceptable deadline yet give individuals control over when to do it.

Core areas (livingroom, bathroom, kitchen, hall) that need a daily frisk as well as a once or twice a week booster could become the total responsibility of one person: the same person would do the everyday frisk and the weekly boosters.

Where there is more than one black belt? Experts divide housework into three main tasks: tidy and clean, meals and laundry. Childcare is the fourth major task, if you have children, and entertaining is a fifth optional activity. These are good workable divisions for sharing housework. One person doing tidying and cleaning, the other doing meals and shopping, and each doing their own laundry is a possibility. But swop around the chores. Homes cannot afford specialists who handle one category of chore only.

'We have friends,' says Liz, 'where the guy is able to do a magnificent garlic and rosemary lamb dish with all the trimmings. But that's all he can do.' Liz and Andrew run their roster for about two months, then they swop around. 'Two months gives us time to get control over our roster,' says Andrew. 'The first week after a changeover is always the hardest!' But they say it benefits their overall housework skills. 'It would be easier to stick to the same jobs all the time, but in the long run that's not the answer. Everyone has to be able to tackle all your home's tasks, difficult spots and all.'

When, as they hope, they have a child, they'll readjust their roster again.

The following pages show a sample and a blank roster. In the latter, the helpers' initials are to be inserted in the boxes, the jobs that your home needs under the headings.

Roster

EVERY DAY'S SIX TASKS	M	T	W	T	F	S	S
EMPTY DISHWASHER							
CHILDCARE –GET UP, DRESS, FEED							
CHILDCARE –SCHOOL RUN							
CHILDCARE –HOMEWORK							
CHILDCARE –BATH/BED							
MAKE LUNCHES							
HELP BEFORE DINNER							
PREPARE AND SERVE DINNER							
FILL AND START DISHWASHER							
KITCHEN CLEAR-UP							
FRISK CORE AREA							
15-MINUTES LAUNDRY							
DAILY GARBAGE							
EVERY WEEK BOOSTERS	**M**	**T**	**W**	**T**	**F**	**S**	**S**
LIVING ROOM							
HALL AND STAIRS							
BATHROOM							
KITCHEN							
BEDROOM(S)							
PUT OUT AND TAKE IN BINS							
SHOPPING							
STOW IT AWAY							
LAUNDRY (OWN OR HOUSEHOLD)							
OUTDOOR WORK (GARDEN, DOG)							
OCCASIONAL/BLITZ JOBS	**M**	**T**	**W**	**T**	**F**	**S**	**S**

BLANK ROSTER

EVERY DAY'S SIX TASKS	M	T	W	T	F	S	S

EVERY WEEK BOOSTERS	M	T	W	T	F	S	S

OCCASIONAL/BLITZ JOBS	M	T	W	T	F	S	S

12
DO YOU NEED HOME HELP?

You would love a multi-purpose helper, an understudy to stand in for you any time anywhere, at the sink, the potty, the PTA meeting.

But that is not the way help comes packaged. Take a package that *is* being offered. Perhaps devise a slightly new-style package. By delegating what can be delegated, you will have made time for yourself to do the remaining tasks. These will vary depending on what help you find. A helper may be great at three out of five things on your wish list, but no good at the others. So they're the ones that you will have to do yourself.

Are you clear whether you need help with housework, with childminding, or a combination of the two?

Before you go looking, anticipate the following points.

THE HOUSE KEY

Am I going to be here always when my helper arrives? And leaves? If not, don't look for someone until you have decided on an arrangement for the key, for payment, and for contact in case of difficulty or just for discussing things. Perhaps Day One could be in the evening or at the weekend when you can meet and agree what's to be done.

This is a big consideration for first-time help seekers. A new awareness of home security is required when you have helpers. Helpers want to be honest and helpful. Make it easy for them. Do not behave carelessly about home security or with your belongings, and don't leave obviously tempting stuff lying around. These precautions are not aimed at your home helper. They are aimed at a wider circle of contacts, to avoid giving the impression that your home is an easy target. Your helper deserves to be protected from suspicion or temptation, and you can best do that by routine prudent security measures.

WHAT IS ON YOUR WISH LIST?

Getting a home help does not mean the end of housework as you've known it. Because housework comes in three thoroughnesses: a frisk, a booster and a blitz once or twice a week, help doing a once or twice a week booster is a common way of organising help. You and your household members do the rest, the daily frisks and the periodic blitzes.

The same chores on each occasion or a list of today's chores each occasion? If you can manage to stick to the same requirements on each occasion, your helper will become quick and efficient at that routine, with minimum input from you. Yes, it may mean that sometimes stuff will be done that doesn't strictly need it. But a changing list is really time-consuming to prepare because you have to inspect and assess your home on each occasion before writing the day's list. And it can be confusing for a helper and result in less work getting done.

If you ask your helper to do the standard, unchanging parts of your housework they'll do that quickest. Rather than spend time demonstrating once-off items to a helper, you and your household members do the odd or occasional jobs.

If your home is too big for the whole of it to be boosted in one session, you'll probably be looking for the following: the busiest or core area of your home will be boosted each session; plus a marginal area, a different marginal area each session in rotation.

Or you could request half-and-half. That is, always do the core area, plus some menu items which you will request on a note on each occasion.

Don't ask for too little. You may think that vacuuming is all that you want done, that you don't mind doing the rest yourself. But there's no point asking for vacuuming only, if the place is going to end up looking vacuumed but sloppy. You really need vacuuming plus a 'look' put on the place.

'Gap-fillers' are useful to have in mind for slack days. Perhaps the children are away for a week so there's less to be done. Or visitors have resulted in your doing some of the work the day before. Or you're all away for two weeks but your helper needs the continuity of income. Periodic tasks could be tackled here: clear out the kitchen presses, just one at a time or all at one go, or clean light fixtures, for example.

What initiatives can your helper take? You want someone with some but not too much initiative until you feel confident about your helper's judgement. It's your agenda that you want carried out, not your helper's agenda.

Standards. It's difficult to convey how thoroughly you like things done. Would you like a few things thoroughly done or a lot of things surface done? A few things boosted or a lot of things frisked? With a new helper, it's really too cumbersome to inspect everything at the end of each session. The quickest method is to plant a few spot tests, make a note of them and check afterwards. Otherwise it's easy to be so busy that you let matters drift.

NEW-STYLE HELP PACKAGES

Supermarket shopping and putting away

I enjoy getting this done – it can be a two or two-and-a-half-hour-a-week task. You could look for a local home-maker to do your supermarket shopping and put it away. It works well if you prepare a master-list of your usual requirements (brand and size). If possible write your list in the sequence of your local supermarket's layout. Make photocopies of it and tick your requirements each week. Yes you need to trust your helper but no, it's not difficult to verify purchases from an itemised supermarket receipt. If they are shopping for more than one person, you'll expect a separate receipt for your items.

Meal preparation for your freezer

A good help, using your recipes or your helper's, packaged in the portion sizes you specify, delivered to your home or collected by you. Or perhaps prepared by your shopper/putter away.

After-school help for your children

Perhaps an older student might accompany them home from school and help with homework until your return.

Outdoor work, gardening, sweeping

You may be able to get someone to come and bring their own equipment – saves you having to be there.

Childminding help

Do you need a daytime childminder who may do some
limited housework? A housework person who may do
some limited childminding? Or an evening babysitter?

But cleaning help is not reorganising help

You cannot expect a helper to rethink your bedroom
layout or tell you how many more pairs of socks you need
for the children. And helpers may not be multi-purpose.
For example, some cleaning people are not good at ironing,
and it would be a mistake to force them! If you need ironing
done, say so in the ad or at the telephone interview.

CHILDMINDERS

For childminding help, have your children present during
some of the interview, to see how they get along. Housework + childcare is a tricky balance to get right. It's
difficult to do a super housework job and a super childcare job at the same time. You're looking for someone who
will be kind to your children.

If you are hiring someone who will spend a lot of time
with your children, find a childcare book whose views you
agree with and get your helper to read it. Most of these
books read persuasively and are non-threatening to
helpers who might have started with other views. Many
parents learn what they know about childcare largely from
books, so why not sitters?

SITTERS

You might like to keep two babysitters on your active list,
so that your children will be used to more than one in
case the first cannot make it. Say this to the sitter, who
will almost certainly understand and perhaps even offer

a friend.

'Darling, let's get a sitter and go out tonight,' sounds like an offer you can refuse! As if 'a' sitter is good enough for *my* kids. 'Let's see if Susan or Rita can babysit tonight so that we could go out,' is a likelier proposition.

Sitters are not surprised to be asked at short notice, though longer notice is better if you know in advance. Sitters also expect to be accompanied home if late, or to stay overnight. They expect to be paid per hour (and a full hour's pay for a fraction of an hour) and paid that night. And they expect to be able to make themselves a snack and to make local phone calls within reason.

Daytime sitters can be a great help. A good arrangement is to find a local student who can come a couple of afternoons a week to do some housework and also be available to babysit some evenings or perhaps daytime at weekends. It gives the student a dependable income and it means that when you are going out, the children know the sitter and you don't have to spend time on The Night organising and arranging your home for a new person.

WITH YOUR CHILDMINDER, DISCUSS TV, TELEPHONE, THEIR FRIENDS CALLING

It's quite OK to say what you consider reasonable. 'I have found it better not, so I'll be asking you not to. Do you have any difficulty with that?' But give definite no-nos only for matters which you consider serious enough to discontinue the employment for if disobeyed.

It's OK to say what TV programmes you are happy for your children to watch, and to specify that the TV should be switched off at other times while your children are up.

Friends calling and coming in for five minutes at going-

'CLEAR UP AFTER YOUR SNACKS.'
'KEEP YOUR BELONGINGS IN YOUR BEDROOM.'

home time, or for an hour, for an evening or overnight? Decide what your attitude is to these various situations and say if you don't want it. My own view is that for evening babysitting, one friend (same sex as your sitter) is OK. But more than one friend can make your child feel a stranger in her own home; and a romantic boyfriend or girlfriend will seldom have the same feeling of loyalty to your family as your sitter. You could say this at the interview. Decide whether you think it a sacking matter if your wishes are not followed.

You're not looking for someone who never makes phone calls, doesn't have friends. But you're looking for a helper who understands that it is not businesslike to bring their social life and relaxation into their business place – your home.

Almost certainly you make personal telephone calls at work from time to time. Your helper may need to do so also, and a short phone call occasionally is acceptable. You work better when that problem is off your mind. Long calls or long-distance calls on your time and on your phone bill are a different matter. After all, you might wish to phone home to enquire about your child or to say you'll be later/earlier than expected. Or you might be expecting an incoming message for yourself. If you are worried about it, try leaving your telephone on answerphone.

Will your helper eat with the family or not? No harm if not. Helpers often prefer a tray in front of the TV.

Drop home unexpectedly from time to time or get a friend or relative to do so. Telephone home to speak to your child. Keep in touch with the vibes.

FINE-TUNING YOUR HELP

Expect to reassess and revise your instructions after a few sessions, and tell your helper to expect this. Perhaps you realise that you've not given sufficiently clear instructions or your helper hasn't got the hang of what you've asked. Or you change your requirements, or an unforseen issue arises. So don't be embarrassed about a review after a few weeks, and tell your helper to expect this. Indeed your helper may welcome the opportunity to clarify matters. It never occurred to me on Day One to say: 'Pease don't vacuum up puppy-poo, even if dry, because it makes the entire vacuum smelly.'

You can say: 'Since you've been coming I've been much better able to see which are the jobs I can get to myself, and which are those that I'd best enjoy someone else doing. So could I ask you to try such and such?'

Or you may have given conflicting messages to your helper. If on one occasion you said: 'Lovely to get all the ironing done,' your helper may feel it necessary to hustle through jobs at a quicker, less thorough pace than you would wish, so as to get all the ironing done next time also. 'It was great to see the grass cut' (cut one slack day) may convey that you would like it cut all the time when you wouldn't. These only become apparent over time, so let there be no embarassment about fine-tuning your arrangement.

Satisfactory help is heart-lifting. Unsatisfactory help is useless, worse than useless. Often it's how you specify what you want that makes the difference! So first decide what you want. Only then can you communicate this to a helper.

Do I have to clear before a helper comes?

It is kind of cartoon stuff, people who clean up before the cleaning person comes. But the family has to do a certain amount so that the helper can get on with the next bits: start the wash so that the clothes are ready to iron, pick up their things so that the house is ready to clean and vacuum. Before cleaning and vacuuming can be done, things have to be picked up and the place made tidy, and that's best done by home dwellers. Newcomers or outsiders will not know what belongs where or what can be thrown out.

There's no point getting a helper to do all frisk items that the family could manage, and none of the booster jobs. So don't feel peevishly that your helper is making you do half the work. Try to look on this effort as a blessing in disguise. Yes, it is a bore and a burden and nags you when you want your home to be a relaxing place. But it forces the housework through. It amounts to your starting the critical path of chores so that your helper can complete them.

The question on day one is: do you clean and tidy the place beforehand so as to show how you like it done? Or do you leave everything sloppy so as to show what needs doing? It's up to you what you think is the best approach.

THE AD, THE PHONE INTERVIEW, THE INTERVIEW

Local ads are best, as they're likely to produce a local helper. Advertise in a local newspaper or perhaps in a college or supermarket. Then use the telephone contact as the first interview. You want to ask questions and give information to see if both you and your caller think that a personal interview is worthwhile.

Write your questions and the information you want to give on a page and make copies of it. Start a different page for each telephone caller. Otherwise it's easy afterwards to be confused and to forget who said what. You can refer to the page during a subsequent personal interview. The page should have:

- Caller's name, address, phone number
- I am looking for someone to come (frequency) for (hours) to do (what?)
- Have you done similar work?
- Are you working at present?
- Do you think the hours would fit your schedule?
- How would you get here?
- I absolutely must have a good timekeeper. I need someone here before I leave. In the event that you couldn't come, is there someone else you could send? Could you let me know at least an hour before the due time?
- When could you start?
- Have you experience of child-minding?
- Have you experience of cooking? What kinds of food?
- Can you iron? May I show you how I like it done?
- Are you a smoker?
- Would you be able to work overtime occasionally, perhaps some evenings or childminding at weekends?
- Are you familiar with an alarm system?
- Do you have a reference from a present or past employer or from school?
- I have other people to call. May I come back to you?

If you are suggesting an interview, ask for references to

be brought. You simply *must* check up on these, so do not glance at them in an embarrassed way and hand them back saying, 'Fine, that's fine'. Bring the references to a table where you have paper and pen, and in a businesslike way, write down the details, name, address, phone number, and dates of employment mentioned. Check the reference. Good applicants have no problems with having references checked. It's a courtesy to suggest to the applicant that they tell their former employer to expect your phone call, so a one- or two-day time lag is appropriate before making the call.

If the references check out, you could phone your applicant to make an offer of employment. This would usually be an offer to go ahead on a three- to four-week trial basis to see if you suit one another; and mention that any uncertainties on either side might be clarified at that time.

13

QUESTIONS YOU MIGHT LIKE TO ASK BEFORE STARTING EQUAL OPPORTUNITIES HOUSEWORK

Q *How soon can we start equal opportunities housework in our home?*

Don't rush into it tonight. You first need to know:

1 Are we talking black, purple, green or yellow belt helpers? Helpers are needed at each level. Yellow belt is the minimum requirement, the beginner's level.

2 Does everyone understand what they are asked to do and how to do it?

3 Is your home set up to be easy to run, and set up for many helpers? Are your how-to systems and methods thought out, set up and known to everyone?

4 Have you drawn up a roster? Purple and black belts do rostered tasks.

5 Do you agree on standards? Everyone's standards vary. This is as hard on the person with low standards as on the person with high standards. Low standards may mean that they are geninely less fussy - or simply less fussy when they are doing the task. 'My partner has very high standards - for everyone else!' Like discussing where to live or how many kids to have to whether

to have a dog, discuss standards. Don't start equal opportunities housework until you've agreed standards (a) for communal areas (b) for personal areas.

6 Decide calmly, before you begin, what penalties are fair for neglecting duties. It is essential to agree this in advance, away from the aggro of the moment. Missed duties can be heartbreaking, emotionally and practically, and are usually taken personally. It's a well known dodge in every human occupation to bungle or to be unreliable so as not to be asked again. It may be a genuine mistake, but that's no consolation. So anticipate hiccups and agree how to deal with them. Perhaps the culprit does double tasks the next day; and if he or she forgets again, quadruple the next day. Discuss. And agree in advance.

7 Name the day. Will it be like give-up-smoking day, with a countdown and a bit of ceremony? Will you start it at a weekend, when everyone is at home? Good luck, men. Good luck, women. Good luck, boys and girls.

Q *How long will it be before equal opportunities housework is running in our home?*

If you and your household are new to the idea of shared housework it could take six months for your system to be up and running.

Six months?

You cannot be serious?

Well, getting the guys to do their bit often fails at the beginning. That's why you need to think of six months before the scheme is working. Six months for the home's

BUT WOULD DOING HOUSEWORK CHANGE HIS
PERSONALITY?
NOT A HOPE, DEAR.

systems to be set up, tasks to be learnt, rosters allocated, misunderstandings sorted out. Six months for CIY habits to become second nature, and for convincing everyone that the scheme is here to stay. It takes time for man and woman to conquer housework.

Q *Would doing housework change my partner's personality?*

Not a hope. Neither your partner's nor your children's personality. We offer our children extra skills in languages, swimming, drama, dance. Housework skills also enhance life.

You do no favour to your partner or kids if you keep them incapable. Many nine-year-olds like the achievement and importance of doing jobs in the home. So do two- to eight-year-olds. It's much better for your partner and kids to spend twenty minutes getting themselves organised than to spend that time looking for their belongings and blaming Mom.

Q *Should kids be paid for housework?*

Not for yellow or green belt stuff. For purple or black belt? If you are at present giving your kids pocket money out of the kindness of your heart and they do the housework out of the kindness of their hearts and it works . . . that's great.

But perhaps it's not working as well as you'd like? Linking pocket money to completed housework could make a difference. Be prepared to inspect the work and insist on the timetable. Withhold payment if necessary. You will have to do this only once or twice.

My children like this method. It's fair. And it gets the work done. However, your children may not need pocket money from you if they earn it outside. You will still need their help at home. It will then be the same housework contribution they would make if they were sharing a home with friends.

If you are prepared to pay for outside help, and your children undertake that work for payment, then paying them will let you insist on high standards.

Yes, you would have to be a firm manager. No, don't pay by the hour; just think of all the interruptions, the phone conversations while the switched-on vacuum makes a busy sound? Pay a rate for the completed task. First, put on your management hat and figure out what a fair rate is.

Stick with your helper the first few times to sort out any uncertainties. Be prepared to inspect the work, and to insist on agreed standards and the agreed timetable.

Q *Is equal opportunities housework unfair?*

Expecting everyone to participate in housework is not unfair. What's unfair is expecting it without notice, or without letting them know in advance what they are to do and when. This dashes their hopes of relaxation or other activities, and takes away their control of their own time.

That's why everyone should know that they're expected to be yellow belt as a minimum. And that's why a roster is necessary for purple and black belts.

Q *My partner and children don't notice what has to be done.*

Some cutie pies don't, truly don't connect housework with themselves. For them it's like listening to someone else's telephone conversation. They may be in the same room but they just know that it doesn't concern them. When they are asked to help, it's as if this is the first they have heard of it, as if this conversation or request had never taken place before.

Getting them to commit to a yellow, green, purple or black belt is the first step. Getting them to stick to it is the next step.

So don't take it personally if it seems slow at first. If the yellow, green, purple or black belt tasks are forgotten, you must not, *must not* step in and do them. Helpers need to see the consequences of duties neglected. Perhaps assign tasks that will have a personal impact if neglected, such as preparing the evening meal, doing the shopping. And agree beforehand on fair penalties for neglected duties.

Q *Since they don't notice, do I have to ask for everything?*

At the beginning, probably yes. But there are good ways to ask, and bad ways.

The good way to ask is the 'almost automatic' way: a minimum of requests gets a maximum of tasks done.

- *A roster* saves asking for the same tasks day after day.
- *Clear-it-yourself* is a good request. It can prevent the following kind of conversation:
  'Please don't leave the knife with chocolate-spread on

the chair.

'And put the bread back in the press.

'And please wash your cup after a snack.

Maeve says 'I know that my daughter used to feel bothered (my mother is always asking me to do things), so I never had the heart to say 'And wipe the table and counter after you.

- Nowadays I just make one request - clear-it-yourself - and my daughter understands that that means doing all the bits of the job, without prompting.'

- *The job, the whole job . . .*

Prepare the vegetables means: 'and leave them clean in a clean pot of water with the peelings disposed of, the sink tidy and the knife put away'.

Clear away after a meal means: 'clear the table and the work surfaces, wash the dishes, sweep the floor and leave the kitchen tidy'.

Vacuum means: 'and put the vacuum away afterwards'.

- *House rules*

'No personal belongings scattered in communal areas' is a house rule that makes sense. It saves a heap of differently phrased reminders that all mean the same thing: 'Don't leave your belongings floating around. Put your schoolbag in your bedroom. Don't leave your sports gear on the kitchen table. Whose are these magazines, toys, sweaters, books? *Hang your coats up*. Everyone should have *some* designated storage space in communal areas. So it is fair to say 'No' to scattered or abandoned personal belongings in communal areas.

THEY SAY THAT PEOPLE WHO ARE HOPELESS AT
HOUSEWORK ARE CHARMING AND
WONDERFUL IN EVERY OTHER WAY.
WHO SAYS THAT?
THE PEOPLE WHO ARE HOPELESS AT HOUSEWORK.

Q   *I've always done all the housework. But now I'ld like to change our system at home. How do I go about it?*

It's OK to say "let's renegotiate". Renegotiate is not a bad word. Do not rake over how unfair it has been in the past. The present and the future are what you want to get right. A good working arrangement may last only twelve to eighteen months before it needs to be adjusted to new home circumstances. So it's never too late to propose an adjustment.

How you get it going will depend on how you generally decide things in your home: noisily or humourously or logically or stealthily. Perhaps with a bit of flattery or bribery?

But if you want a change, *you* must change first. If you have been doing everything, this has sent two messages to household members:

- It is in capable hands.
- None of the rest of you can do it properly.

Capable housekeepers may be their own worst enemy. Nobody else in their home feels that they could be as good. And the more effortless you make it seem, the less help you'll get.

Perhaps what's needed is a bit of under-par performance from you? There's nothing like a few ruined--in-the-wash favourite garments or a few late, cold or non-existent meals to convince people that they would be better off doing it themselves.

Bungle a job is a well-known dodge in every human occupation. Can you turn it to your advantage, and become the bungler?

MOM, LET GO OF THE HOUSEWORK.
IT DOESN'T BELONG TO YOU.

You got the job, the responsibility, through being reliable. It may be that you'll lose part of the job only by being unreliable. So it may become necessary to let the dinner burn, the house plants die, before the others realise that you're not infallible. Let go of the housework. It does not belong to you. But unless and until you let it go it will belong to you.

While everyone is learning, you must not complain about mistakes, or re-do jobs. If you do, you're half-way to reassuming the entire work yourself.

Q *What is the bottom line? Exactly what housework contribution is required from everyone?*

Housework requirements are remarkably similar from home to home. And the helping hands required are remarkably similar also - so much so that they can almost be standardised:

Everyone chooses a belt. Yellow belt is the minimum. Green, purple or black would be better.

Everyone agrees to clear-it-yourself, clean-it-yourself.

'It's not because I'm mad at you or in a bad mood that I'm suggesting these tasks. It's because minute for minute of housework time, these contributions offer the best value. Not alone does the task get done in the least timewhen it's done by the person on the spot but when it is done immediately, it keeps the place looking good for the longest possible time.'

These days, home dwellers increasingly follow individual timetables for comings and goings and for meals and snacks. Who better to clear away than each individual for himself/herself? Impossible to timetable anyone else to stand by to do it.

An advantage of equal opportunities housework is this: if nobody shirks their own clearup, there will be no build-up, no backlog for others. Backlogs have a domino effect: if tasks have been shirked they become daunting for the next person. And tasks that are daunting will in turn be shirked . . . building up to a big daunting backlog.

Another advantage of equal opportunities housework is that it sets a limit and shows helpers where they stand. Helpers often fear that if they start helping, there will be no stopping. But properly organised, equal opportunities housework need not be a bottomless pit for helpers. Choose and agree the level of help you'll give and you'll know where you stand. You'll be able to get on with your tasks without any wary hedging, and without having to be asked for every short portion of every short task.

Q *What about unlisted tasks?*

The following tasks appear to be top secret, because nobody every notices that they need doing. Try to notice these and other similar unlisted tasks. Don't wait to be asked to do them:

- Replace the light bulb when the old one is finished.
- Replace the toilet roll when the old one is finished.
- And the kitchen paper.
- Give a hand bringing in the groceries and putting them away.
- Notice that the floor needs sweeping.

- Pick up and tidy after a dog has scattered the rubbish.
- Defrost the fridge or freezer.
- Empty full waste-baskets.
- Tidy/clear the kitchen. Even when everyone has done their one-person portion of kitchen clearance, it still often leaves a 35-minute clearup.

Q *How can my partner and children learn to do the housework?*

Wanted housekeepers, no experience necessary.

It's true. Everybody begins somewhere, makes mistakes, learns from their mistakes.

Whose Housework Is It Anyway? does not contain detailed instructions on cleaning methods or appliances. Great instructions are already available, supplied with the appliances and with cleaning products. They enable helpers to be independent of mother, to do a teach-yourself job.

This helps everyone to bond with their tasks, 'take ownership' of them – very important, according to workplace experts.

If they really ask to be shown, for example, the yellow, green, purple, black proficiency tests – make a meal, do the laundry, or clean the bathroom, choose a teaching time when neither you nor your helper is in a hurry.

Everyone knows that it's quicker to do a job yourself than to have to coax or nag others, instruct them and inspect the job afterwards. That is especially true when you're in a hurry. So don't wait until you're in a hurry. Instruct when neither you nor your helper is rushed.

Your family will not do good housework without experience. They will not gain experience without first doing bad housework. The Chinese proverb says

I see – I understand

I do – I learn.

AND I DEDICATE THIS BOOK TO MY FAMILY,
WITHOUT WHOM IT WOULD HAVE BEEN
COMPLETED MUCH SOONER.